The Most Compelling Adventure

John Starr

Copyright © 2019 by John Starr

The moral right of the author has been asserted.
All rights reserved. No part of this publication may be reproduced, stored in a retrieval system, or transmitted, in any form or by any means, without the prior permission in writing of the publisher, nor be otherwise circulated in any form of binding or cover other than that in which it is published and without a similar condition including this condition being imposed on the subsequent publisher.

ISBN 978-1-9164811-1-4

A CIP catalogue record for this book is available from the British Library.

Iheringius
An imprint of
Joensuu Media Ltd
20-22 Wenlock Road
London
N1 7GU
England

iheringius.com

I dedicate this work of worship (labour of love) to Jesus, the Great Heart of my own heart, my Soul Survivor, Restorer, Replenisher and Travel Companion in the great and most compelling adventure of all. Your friendship, Jesus, has continued to be incalculable, indomitable and irresistible. To say "Thank you for being my Friend" seems so inadequate compared to the towering majesty of your awesome love and sovereign patience. Thank you for your inspirational words to me, "Be still. Do not be afraid. I am with you". It is an honour to be invited to walk with you. I hope you get pleasure from this small and incomplete offering. I also hope it helps and encourages my brothers and sisters in Christ in their lifelong adventure with you.

Contents

Acknowledgements		7
Preface		9
The Ways of God		11
1	Christ in You	23
2	The Bridegroom God	35
3	Called by Love	47
4	Responding to the Caller	59
5	The School of the Spirit	69
6	Wrestled by God	89
7	The Way of Silence and Stillness	101
8	Asking Good Questions	117
9	The Wilderness School	131
10	The God Who Hides and Reveals	149
11	Perspective Is Everything	165
12	Beyond the Last Mountain	179
References		195
Authors in Alphabetical Order		199
Flyleaf		203

Acknowledgements

I am so grateful to Lynette, my life-long travel-companion, and other family members for their encouragement and patience shown me in writing this book. I owe a great debt of gratitude to the influences of such godly men as Revd Alan Harrison (my first spiritual director) and Graham Cooke (Brilliant Book House). I am grateful to God for putting Marko Joensuu in my path at exactly the right time and for his belief in me and encouragement to complete the process.

To the number of believers over the years who embarrassed me by insisting I should write books, thank you, and I hope now you are satisfied!

Preface

I have always been fascinated by the ways of God, particularly his paradoxical ways. His logic seems so contrary to the ways of the world. In God's ways of doing things, down is up, darkness is a blinding light, vulnerability is strength, loss is gain, death is the portal to life, surrendering is the path to victory. Much that our society disdains is exalted by God. Suffering is a precursor to splendour, pressure produces godliness, and adversity prepares the way for advancement.

Not everything in the world that glistens is gold. In contrast, in the kingdom of God, not everything that is gold might initially seem to glisten! In the ways of the Spirit of God, treasure is to be found in the muck and mire of our lives. The Spirit of God comes to illumine our lives, yet in his wisdom he can sometimes choose to come to us in disguise, hidden, withdrawing into silence, and even appearing to abandon us. Friendship with God does not mean life will be made easier or more comfortable. Quite the contrary! God's friendship can appear ambiguous, and we are hard pressed to ask why, as often we can't see the gold at all.

All the ways of the Lord are loving and wise. It is to our benefit to learn his ways so that we can be reassured and encouraged, saving ourselves from unnecessary bewilderment and pain. We shall find ourselves not misinterpreting and wrestling against God's purposes but recognising and embracing his wise and loving will. The selection of themes in this book reflects many of my own experiences, having been captivated and enthralled for most of my life by His Majesty, the Lord Jesus Christ. He is my life, the reason I live and not simply exist. He is the air I breathe, my very soul, the Great Heart of my own heart.

In this book I have endeavoured to explain some of these enigmatic ways, and, hopefully, it will reassure and strengthen you in the pursuit of the Lord's friendship and his pursuit of your personal spiritual growth and development.

God meant it for good.

Introduction

The Ways of God

The ways of the Lord are right; the righteous walk in them, but the rebellious stumble in them.[1]

Life is an adventure and the journey with the Source of all life is the greatest, most compelling and satisfying adventure of all. It is about exploring and discovering more and more of God and how he defines and shapes our lives. Each step of the way in this adventure beckons us to go deeper in our friendship with him. Every time the Lord leads us into a new phase of the journey, it is meant to expand our understanding of him and deepen our love, joy, and peace in the Holy Spirit. Each season is designed to give us a fresh and more powerful vision of God and cause us to gain a breakthrough into a new dimension of life in the Spirit. He wants to lead us through experience after experience to transform us into his own likeness, advancing from glory to glory.

> Now the Lord is the Spirit, and where the Spirit of the Lord is, there is freedom. And we all, with unveiled face, beholding the glory of the Lord, are being transformed into the same image from one degree of glory to another. For this comes from the Lord who is the Spirit.[2]

After many years of enjoying an intimate friendship and exciting

---

1   Hosea 14:9 NIV
2   2 Corinthians 3:17-18 English Standard Version Anglicised

adventures with God, which many would envy, Moses made what seems a strange request of God. "Teach me your ways so that I may know you."[3] How perplexing! If we had been there, we might have asked, "But Moses, the Lord speaks to you face to face, as a man speaks with his friend.[4] With all God's personal encounters with you and your supernatural experiences of the Exodus and Sinai, why would you think you need to ask God to educate you in his ways, in order that you may know him and find favour with him? Surely, you already know more of God than anyone of your time! As for God's favour, haven't you already received it by the bucketload?"

For all Moses' experiences of God, his request strongly suggests that he realised there was far more of God to discover. He understood that to know God fully we need not only to understand his will but also comprehend his ways. The ways of God are the application, the strategies, by which he implements his will. They are the activity of his wisdom. If the will of God could be described as the destination, then his ways are the journeys we are intended to take to reach it. Our Father's desire is to bring us to maturity in Christ. That is his will. He employs various means to accomplish his plan. He will use times and seasons, tests and trials, subtlety and secrecy, hiddenness and manifestation, pressure and silence. But we can trust that he always has our best interest in his heart.

> And we know that in all things God works for our good of those who love him and have been called according to his purpose.[5]

As Joseph declared, "God meant it for good."[6] This calls for wisdom on God's part and discernment from us. When we recognise and cooperate with his ways, it brings peace, favour and rest. Ignorance of his ways and resistance bring only confusion, restlessness and harm.

3	Exodus 33:13
4	Exodus 33:11 NIV
5	Romans 8:28
6	Genesis 50:20

The Ways of God

My people are destroyed from lack of knowledge.[7]

Let us delve deeper into the Scriptures to see the implications of Moses' request. Moses said to God, "If you are pleased with me, teach me your ways so I may know you and continue to find favour with you." The Hebrew word for favour is *rason*, and it can also be translated as "goodwill", "acceptance", "pleasure" or "blessings heaped upon a person." Its New Testament Greek equivalent is *charis*, which means grace, but it also includes a sense of favour being bestowed upon someone.[8]

The Lord replied, "My Presence will go with you, and I will give you rest."[9] The Old Testament Hebrew word for "rest" is *nuah*, and it includes the idea of being quiet, still. Its Greek parallel in the New Testament is *anapausis*, which means "refreshment", "rest", "enjoying fellowship with God", "settled", "stable" and "to be still and at peace", and it is related to the Sabbath rest of God in Hebrews 4:9-10. Its antithesis is restless, unsettled, unstable and out of fellowship with God.

The Lord also promised, "I will cause all my goodness to pass in front of you."[10] Knowing the ways of God enables us to see at a deeper level what God is like and who he wants to be for us. Such knowledge will cause us to enter his majestic presence and experience more of his indomitable love for us. We can appreciate his active goodness in our lives at a more profound level and rest in the amazing refreshment, stability and confidence it brings.

To know God's ways is to know his eternal goodness. To enter God's rest does not imply we become inactive, but it implies that God becomes active. As Jesus says,

> Come to me all who are weary and burdened, and I will give you rest [refresh you]. Take my yoke upon you and learn from me, for I am gentle and humble in heart, and you will find rest for your souls. For my yoke is easy and my burden is light.[11]

---

7   Hosea 4:6
8   For example, Luke 1:28 uses words "highly favoured".
9   Exodus 33:14
10   Exodus 33:19
11   Matthew 11:28-29

The Bible says that though Israel knew the deeds of God, Moses knew the ways of God.[12] We can experience God in action and observe his works without fully understanding his deeper purpose behind the events. Jesus was often faced with this ignorance in response to his preaching and miracles, even among his own followers.[13] Moses' greatest achievement was his intimacy with God. To know God personally is to attain to the highest honour given to humanity. Yet, we cannot truly know God if we do not know his ways, if we are not knowledgeable of his heart motives and intimate with the secrets of his passions. To know God and his ways is to be amazed at the resolve of his love, the compulsion of his goodness and his attraction to the humble.

The evidence of Scripture declares the ways of God are perfect, holy, just, righteous, loving and faithful.[14] David was known to God as a man after his own heart. His experience of God's ways led him to write,

> As for God, his way is perfect [does not fail] . . . It is God who arms me with strength and makes my way perfect.[15]

Because David appreciated that God's ways are flawless and do not fail, he walked in God's ways, and his way did not fail but thrived.

The ways of God are the means by which he deals with us, and what he wants to do in us. His ways are the choices he makes concerning us. God said, "Jacob have I loved, but Esau have I hated."[16] Loving Jacob was God's *choice*. We may reason that the way Esau was treated seems unjust. After all, Jacob had behaved badly toward his brother, cheating him of his birth-right, yet on closer inspection we find that Esau despised his spiritual birth-right and in so doing he had dishonoured God.

12	Psalm 103:7
13	Matthew 16:5-12
14	Deuteronomy 32:4, Psalms 25:10, 77:13, 145:17, Hosea 14:9
15	Psalm 18:30, 32
16	Romans 9:13

God tells us that his ways are higher than our ways.[17] He has his own determined way, and there is no room for anyone else's choices. He deals with one person in one way and with another person in another way. God's ways are what he considers best, and they imply that he acts according to what makes him happy. No one can tell him how he should act. He has no need of an advisory board to tell him how to run the universe. He does what pleases him. The ways of God are his choices: he wants to do things one way and not another. He wants to accomplish this matter at this time and not something else. He wants us to encounter this situation but not that one. These are the ways of God.

David asked God, "Show me your ways, O Lord".[18] The Hebrew word for "way" used in this verse is *derek*. Literally, it means "my way", "bent", or "tendency". It was an archer's term. Hunters or soldiers of that day did not receive a standard issue bow and arrow with wires and buttons to adjust the bow to the man. Rather, each marksman went out and found his own piece of wood, and crafted it carefully into a bow. Since each bow was made of different kinds of wood with varying strength and levels of moisture, it was likely that it took days to learn the unique bent and tendency of the wood. Only then could a marksman be accurate with the bow. The word *derek* refers to the process of learning the wood. God is saying to us: "I have specific ways I want you to follow, but to be successful you have to know the unique strengths and qualities of these ways. It will take some time, so plan on investing that time."

Understanding how the Lord desires to work in our lives will help us to increase in his grace and favour. It is, then, not surprising that God's ways can seem strange, enigmatic, paradoxical and even contradictory, alien. When we are going through a fiery ordeal and God is silent or hidden, it can seem quite contradictory to our notion of God. But his ways are

---

17   Isaiah 55:9
18   Psalm 25:4 NKJV

higher and greater than ours.[19] They are the outworking of his benevolent but inscrutable wisdom.

A review of the Bible, and particularly the New Testament, can lead us to the conclusion that God enjoys paradoxes. A paradox is two seemingly contradictory statements which nevertheless express a truth. For example, in the kingdom of God the way down is the way up (Joseph), we have to die to live, loss is the way to gain (Job) and emptiness is the way to fullness. God's nature seems paradoxical to us. While he is consistent in his nature and character, he is unpredictable in his ways. He is unchanging in who he is and wants to be for us. He remains the same, whatever the circumstance. He is consistently good all the time. Therefore, we find him to be utterly dependable, trustworthy and reliable. Yet he is unpredictable in the ways he implements his will and applies it to our lives. Gideon's army of thirty-two thousand was vastly outnumbered by the enemy, and in the natural chances of victory were very slim indeed. Yet God's way was to order Gideon to reduce his fighting force to a mere three hundred, with odds against of a thousand to one. How is that for wisdom! It seems utterly nonsensical! Likewise, when Israel was enslaved by the most occultic and militarily powerful empire on earth, God's way was to send Moses, a geriatric with a stick and a stammer. How bonkers is that! The ways of the Spirit can appear irrational, nonsensical and even madness to the ways of the flesh. But God's way is to display his power and wisdom in weakness and fragility. Life in the realm of the Spirit can be an exciting adventure, even scary at times, but it is definitely not dull. When walking with God, we must be on our guard against assumption and presumption.

What we can be sure about is that everything God does is motivated by love.

> The Lord is righteous in all his ways and loving toward all he has made.[20]

---

19   Isaiah 55:8-9
20   Psalm 145:17

His chief concern is our welfare. This is the key to recognising and appreciating the mysteries of his wisdom and the implementation of his ways.

Much that God could do by his power he prefers to do by his wisdom. There are many things he could do without us by his sovereign power, but he prefers to do them in partnership with us, even though it requires risk and patience. A mother could do a far better job at baking a cake on her own without her little children's helping hands. Involving her children is messier and likely to produce less perfect results, but greater rewards will be achieved: bonding, nurturing and the promotion of the children's personal formation within the context of family. After all, the word "family" comes from the root word "familiar". Risks will be contemplated: the spillage and wastage of ingredients, the mess in the kitchen and the quality of the finished product, as well as the mother's own patience and perseverance. Yet, it would be a work of love. The mother's focus will not be so much on the cake but on the child. The mother withholds her power in order to bond with and nurture her child. Her delight is not in the cake but in the pleasure and satisfaction it gives her child. What God can do by his sovereign power he prefers to do by his wisdom! He delights in seeing the progress we make in growing and maturing in our fellowship with him. *Be fruitful. Increase. Fill. Subdue. Rule.* All that God does is for his pleasure, and his pleasure is directed toward our bonding and personal development.

Because God is always consistent in who he is and who he wants to be for us, our sense of security is to be founded upon his dependability and trustworthiness. His immutable nature means he will never act in contradiction to his nature, even though at times his actions will appear unfamiliar and enigmatic to us.

In God's wisdom, he has designed seasons of spiritual growth and fruitfulness to take place in the least expected location, the desert. The place of spiritual aridity and emptiness is designed to be the prelude to growth in greater intimacy, dependency and personal development.

In the desert, prepare the way of the Lord.[21]

Dark nights of the soul foster receptivity to greater enlightenment. God can appear to us as remote, hidden and withdrawn, but his purpose is to nurture greater desire and intimacy with him. Absence makes the heart grow fonder. His silences can be most eloquent, promoting greater listening and attentiveness within us and preparing us for an upgrade in our ability to recognise and hear his voice in our lives. Spiritual blindness can lead to greater reflection, deeper contemplation and open our eyes to see more acutely in the realm of the Spirit. Faith is tempered and made stronger when it is lived in the dark. Faith grows and matures under pressure. Paul's blindness resulted from seeing the truth of Jesus on the road to Damascus. Although in Paul's case the blindness was physical, its true nature was spiritual in purpose. It triggered a period of greater reflection and spiritual receptivity, opening his spiritual eyes to the truth about himself and the reality of Christ, which he had been blind to. The scales fell from his eyes when he was ready to be filled with the Holy Spirit.

Rest can be an incubator for greater activity and interaction with God. The command from God is:

> Be still, and know that I am God . . . In repentance and rest is your salvation, in quietness and trust is your strength . . . Those who wait upon the Lord shall renew their strength. They shall mount up with wings as eagles; they shall run and not grow weary, and they shall walk and not faint.[22]

Rest is an active waiting on God and the prelude to more productive activity, allowing the Lord to be more active within us. Listening lies at the heart of making progress in a personal relationship with God.

A traumatic, emotional "cul-de-sac" experience can be God's appointment for new direction in our lives. Elijah's depression and withdrawal, even with thoughts of ending it all, was used

---

21   Isaiah 40:3 NIV
22   Psalm 46:10, Isaiah 30:15, 40:31

by God to give him fresh vision and open a new chapter to his ministry. Man's disappointments become God's appointments. The training ground for God's prophetic people is the PIT. God planned the PIT as the way to the palace for Joseph. The PIT stands for a "prophet in training"! The way down is the way up for God's people.

God speaks most eloquently through his silences. His periods of deliberate silence, when he presses the pause button in our lives, can be times when he is waiting for us to make the next move in a process of dialogue and enquiry. God desires partners and the way of mutuality. So often, he operates in a process of dialogue and questioning.

> Ask, and it will be given to you; seek and you will find; knock and it will be opened to you.[23]

We need to learn the language of God's silences if we are to become effective and productive in our walk with him. Seasoned prophetic people are familiar with God's method of questions and answers. His way is to operate by encounter, dialogue and exchange. Often, God will show us something, but not everything, in that moment. He requires us to do some digging; to dig deeper, below the surface of his *rhema* words.[24] He waits for us to come back to him and ask questions about what we are seeing and hearing. On the basis of our asking, he will reveal more. Other times, he takes the initiative in asking the questions, with the sole intent of compelling us to dig deeper into his revelation. Authentic dreams and visions from God can be highly symbolic, engaging in enigmatic metaphorical language. Our job is to refer back to God and ask questions for interpretation and application. Through this approach he is teaching us the value of dependency and submission, saving us from starting successfully in the Spirit but ending up wrongly in the flesh, moving away

---

23   Matthew 7:7
24   *Rhema* literally means an utterance. Examples are found in Luke 1:38, 3:2, 5:5, and Acts 11:16. A *rhema* is a verse or portion of Scripture that the Holy Spirit brings to our attention with application to a current situation or need for direction.

from authentic revelation to carnal assumption and presumption. Peter was sternly rebuked by Jesus when he made this mistake.[25] Progressive and developmental revelation is often released on the basis of asking right questions. Doors are intentionally opened when we learn to knock. Knocking is God's method of teaching us to interact and partner with his authority and power. It can also draw out from us the creativity God has placed within us.

Everything God does serves one clear objective: to draw us into a lasting, loving and dependent friendship with him. It will enrich and transform us, reversing the destructive UDI, the universal declaration of independence, we inherited from Adam. God is everything we need. The cross of Jesus is a plus sign. God is the God of addition, not subtraction. Everything he does is aimed to increase us, not diminish us. Christ is in us, the hope of glory!

The journey of faith will always take us into previously uncharted territory, not unknown to the Bible and the history of the Church, but unknown to our previous experience and understanding of God's ways. This calls for a pioneer spirit, breaking new ground in the life of the Spirit and navigating unfamiliar landscapes, where our security is to be found in trusting ourselves to God's unchanging nature and his constant love toward us. The friends of God are drawn into his confidences.[26]

To know God and his ways is the most exciting and compelling adventure of all.

> And now, O Israel, what does the Lord your God require of you but to fear the Lord your God, to walk in all his ways, to love him.[27]

---

25 Mark 8:29-33
26 John 15:15
27 Deuteronomy 10:12 NIV

Prayer

Lord, teach me your ways.
I want to know more of you and your ways.
I want to follow the adventure of this life in your company,
exploring and discovering more and more of you
and how you desire to define and shape my life.
With each step of the way upon this journey,
you ever beckon me to rise higher in my relationship with
you—to enjoy elevated and exalted living.[28]
I know that all your ways, both obvious and paradoxical, are
loving and wise.
Illuminate my life in whatever ways you see fit,
only let me perceive the unique strengths and qualities of
these ways,
so that with each step I can freely and trustingly say
"Father, into your hands I commit my spirit."
I know this adventure will take some time,
so I plan on investing that time,
all the time you give me.

---

[28] Ephesians 2:6

1

Christ in You

Surely, the Lord is in this place, and I was not aware of it.[29]

Our journey through this life is always in the company of another. We are never alone and sometimes the reality of this truth is made known to us in surprising and breathtaking ways. "The Lord is with you" is a refrain frequently repeated in the Scriptures. The adventure of this life is always a journey of two friends. Jesus says, "Surely I am with you always."[30]

A Daytime Visitation

Alone in the house, the boy was sitting quietly, pondering. All was still. Suddenly he felt a presence enter the room. It silently walked up to him, and, with each step, it grew in intensity. Without any exchange of words, the identity of the presence was immediately disclosed. It was Jesus. The Lord approached the boy, as if there was a silent agreement between them. With increasing intensity, the presence of the Lord drew close to the boy, and then, stepped right inside him. The boy was gripped by an explosion of ecstatic, unearthly, perfect love, which suffused and irradiated every fibre of his being. Never had he experienced such a thing before. It was like a detonation of superhuman love bursting within him. His spirit, enfolded by the presence of

---

29   Genesis 28:16 NIV
30   Matthew 28:20

Christ, seemed to take flight from his body, transported upwards in a rapture of love to ever higher realms of purity and bliss. He had the impression of being borne aloft on the wings of an eagle, and a knowing came to him of the Holy Spirit.

As he was being swept ever higher, without knowing how, he knew he was being taken up toward God the Father. He experienced the strangest mixture of sensations: powerful love enfolding and invading him and yet a growing sense of immense distance before him, as of being on the edge of infinity.

The closer he was drawn toward the Father, the more he was impacted with God's infinite otherness. Although he was experiencing overwhelming love, he also sensed the awesome immensity of God's immortality and holiness, and the smallness of his own mortality. He had the strangest sense of both the nearness and farness—the immanence and transcendence—of the divine presence. He was experiencing God in such rapturous intimacy, and yet, at the same time, God was utterly above and beyond everything.

No words were spoken, no sounds heard, except the boy's own gasping in repeated adoration, *"Abba! Abba!"* This word was not familiar to him at the time.

The power of the presence was becoming so intense that it was making it difficult for the boy to breathe. Hyperventilating, he became alarmed that his body would not be able to sustain the intensity, and his heart would fail. With laboured breath he managed to gasp a plea, "Leave me, Lord, or I will die." Immediately, but with such gentleness, the Lord responded to the boy's plea and began to withdraw, leaving the boy bereft and tear-stained. It was a decision the boy would regret for the rest of his life. The encounter would leave a brand mark upon his soul, forever scarring him with a desire for more of Jesus. The boy made the decision to attend church and give his life to Christ in a public act of dedication.

> For whom He foreknew, He also predestined to be conformed to the image of His Son.[31]

---

31 Romans 8:29 NKJV

Christ in Us, the Hope of Glory

God's universal plan has been and will always be to transform us into the likeness of his Son. His abiding desire is to unite humanity with himself, a sublime union where humanity is exalted to partake of the divine nature,[32] the mortal united with the immortal,[33] the finite with the infinite, the unholy embraced by the holy. God is continually at work in his creation, and he is supremely active in the pinnacle of his creation, humanity. His passion is to fashion and transform us into the likeness of his beloved divine Son, Jesus Christ. It is a labour of passionate and unconditional love. In that love, God refuses to impose his will on us. His gift of free will allows us the freedom to choose for or against him. Salvation and subsequent formation are always matters of choice.

Jesus is God's Prototype Man, the Alpha and Omega, the Sole Original and Final Becoming for all humanity. All of time is inexorably moving toward history's Omega Point, the Perfect Man-God, Christ Jesus, who shall consummate and unite all things together in heaven and earth in himself. He is the Convergence and Consummation for the entire cosmos. He is the Cosmic Christ. Yet each human being must choose for himself whether or not to be part of this "great and final becoming", the ultimate step to existence. Being exalted to the highest state of existence is never automatic or universal; it is dependent upon every soul's decision about Jesus.

Identification with Christ

The more we allow ourselves to be formed into the Prototype Image of Jesus, the more we will resemble him. This is essentially an internal work; we are changed from the inside out. When God came to earth, he did something incredible. He united himself with humanity. He identified himself with the human condition, so that we would be identified with him. Christ became incarnate of the Virgin Mary and dwelt among human

---

32   2 Peter 1:4
33   1 Corinthians 15:53

beings as one of us. Yet, his intention has always been to extend his incarnation to many, taking up residence in each soul, as they give their lives to him. Christ in you, and you in Christ! A divine exchange takes place: our lives for his life. When we give our lives to him, the power of the Most High graciously and wonderfully overshadows us, and the Spirit of the risen Christ comes again to take up residence within us. In our hearts he makes his home. Every authentic believer becomes a Christ-carrier, an embodiment of his life-giving presence inhabiting him or her.[34] Because he lives within us, we live.

> I no longer live, but Christ lives in me. The life I now live in the body, I live by faith in the Son of God, who loved me and gave himself for me.[35]

"Christ lives in me", his union with us, brings us to a tremendous truth, which, if fully grasped, would revolutionise our lives. He took on our identity, and we have taken on his. We can appreciate the power of Jesus' identification with us, yet how much do we recognise and appreciate the power of our identification with him? We may draw encouragement and strength from the fact that in becoming one with us he identified with our whole human existence, including our sin and death. Yet the divine exchange also means we are identified with all that Jesus was and did. As he is the Son of God, we have become sons of God. We share in his identity. Obviously he is God and we are not, yet there are undeserved privileges made possible to us by his Holy Spirit dwelling within us. When Jesus died on the cross, we actually died there with him. Galatians 2:20 begins with "I have been crucified with Christ."[36] Those who are joined to Christ are actually and really crucified with him. We were present in Adam when he sinned, and we were present in Christ when he died and rose again.[37] When Jesus died on the cross, we died there with him. All our sins and their effects died there with him. He took

---

34	Ephesians 5:30 NKJV
35	Galatians 2:20 NIV
36	NIV
37	Romans 5:17

us and all our sins and sorrows into himself. We were in Christ on the cross; our sins were in him, and when he died, we and all our sins died there with him. He did it with us in him.

One with Christ means we are not only one with him in his death, but we are also one with him in his resurrection and exaltation.

> For if we have become identified with him [*sumphotos* is translated "identified with, united with, one with"] in the likeness of his death, certainly we shall also be in the likeness of his resurrection.[38]

When Jesus rose again from the dead, we actually rose to a new life with him. God "made us alive together with Christ."[39] Our bodies are yet to die, but they will experience being raised and glorified in the future. Even so, our resurrection is not limited to that. Our resurrection in Christ has a present application: our spirits have already been raised from death to life. We are alive in Christ!

When he ascended into heaven, we ascended with him and we are seated with him in the heavenly places, sharing in his victory and heavenly authority.[40] This will have ramifications on how we live with our circumstances: above them or under them.

> If then you were co-raised with Christ, seek those things which are above, where Christ is sitting at the right hand of God.[41]

"With Christ" means we are with him in his death and resurrection and with him in his exalted state with the Father. Jesus' truth is our truth. As he is, so are we in this world.[42] Christ in us, the hope of glory!

Our union with Christ also grants us union with his earthly life. The Father has willed that all that belongs to Christ belongs to us. If we were united with Christ in his death and

---

38 Romans 6:5
39 Ephesians 2:5
40 Ephesians 2:6
41 Colossians 3:1
42 1 John 4:17

resurrection, then we were also united with Christ in his earthly life: in his victory over temptation, his supernatural ministry and the authority he carried from his baptism in the Holy Spirit. We have become partakers of his earthly life and ministry because we are in him. If that is true, then when Jesus healed the sick and cast out demons, we were "in him". When he multiplied the loaves and fishes, we were in him. We are not divine. Only Jesus is God, but we are present with him in the heavenly places, with delegated authority from him to act in his name as his ambassadors. He is in us in our earthly state, and we are in him in his heavenly state.

Earth was always made to touch heaven. Heaven has always desired to be united with earth, with humans made in the image of God as his go-betweens. The Creator has always wanted to be united with his creation. Since the cross of Christ, there has been a permanent ladder established between heaven and earth —Jesus. He has broken down all walls. Heaven has come down, and it has come down to raise earth to heaven. Heaven is open. There exists now a constant commerce between heaven and earth, ascending and descending on that ladder, uniting the divine and the human. Heaven is open, and earth is the beneficiary.

The Bible says that as husband and wife become one through marriage, so too does Christ become one with us through his covenant relationship with us. We are married to Jesus. Now he is our Bridegroom God. We are incorporated into the Bride of Christ, and daily we are being drawn to become progressively like our Bridegroom, talking and acting like him, one with him. What a glorious wonder! Jesus is in us and we are in him. As we discern what he desires, we become the vessel of honour through which he continues to present himself to the world.

To proclaim that Christ is in us is to declare that all he was and all that he is, his earthly life as well as his heavenly state, dwell gloriously within us. What a glorious and incredible truth! Words cannot adequately express the amazingly generous goodness and loving kindness of our God. What an undeserved privilege! What an unmerited honour! So undeserved! It is all grace upon grace upon grace. May the

Holy Spirit make this powerful, life-changing truth real to our experience!

All that belongs to Jesus belongs to us. We are identified with him. When the Father looks at us, he sees his Son; he sees us in Christ. Christ took on our identity, and we have taken on his identity.

Our union with Christ has implications for how we appropriate our identity from him and apply his victory to our lives and the lives of others. Truth needs to be worked out in our lives. This is the work of formation into Christlikeness prioritised for us by the Holy Spirit.

The believer's spirit becomes a temple of the divine presence. From the day of new birth, every succeeding day the Spirit of God is active within, labouring to develop and mature us into the full stature of Christ. The Spirit of God will use everything at his disposal to draw us and shape us into the people he wants us to become. There will be times when his ways appear mysterious, paradoxical, and even contradictory. He works in the dark as well as in the light, in secret as well as in the open.[43] At times he will speak plainly, but at other times he will speak with "dark sayings" and enigmatic speech.[44] He will manifest himself to us on mountain-tops, but in other times he may lead us into dark valleys and Gethsemanes. He will lead us beside still waters and other times direct us into the boat headed for stormy waters. While seasons of plenty and fruitfulness will be ordained for us, there will be other times when he will seek to call us into desert places. There will be times when he will lift us high in the sight of others, but only after he has lowered us into a pit of preparation. The way down is the way up. There are times to enjoy, and there are times to endure. Pressure is a common instrument in God's hand to produce godliness in us. Testing and trials are common in the process of formation into Christlikeness. We grow most in times of pressure. Everything the Spirit of God does in us is not to diminish but to increase and prosper us. Pressure is only the

---

43   Psalm 139:12, Luke 24:15-16, 28, Mark 6:48b. Luke 24:28 puts it as "acted as if he were going farther". Greek *prosepoiesato* often means "pretend".
44   Numbers 12:8

loving touch of the Master Potter's hands sculpting and shaping our clay into vessels of honour. When we keep our eyes on Jesus, all the tests and trials become for us our grace growers, instead of foes to resist and war against. Butterflies are never freed from the cocoon without a struggle. There is a struggle that makes us strong, and not only strong but also more like Christ.

But ignorance of his ways will lead to wrong assumptions, anxiety, and loss of hope. The prophet Hosea said, "My people perish through lack of knowledge."[45]

Signposts in the Landscape

Knowing God's ways will lead us on the path to ultimate victory and success. Our destiny is to be formed into the full stature of Christ. There are some indispensable signposts to follow in the school of the Holy Spirit, particularly when times of hard testing and fiery trials beset us along the predetermined path God has set for us. Remember, the Potter uses a kiln as an essential part of the process to completing the pot!

The first signpost is learning to discern God as the source. When we are unaware of God's ways, we can be mistaken in believing the circumstances we experience are either the enemy at work or our own sin paying us back. However, there are times when the real source of them is God, and we cannot cast him out or take authority over him! What we are experiencing is the will of God, and he has personally engineered a situation to grow and increase us in favour and authority. Instead of resisting and waging war, we are meant to embrace the Spirit's process and yield in expectant faith to it as a grace grower in our lives.

The second signpost is learning to acknowledge the superiority of God's wisdom and love. The overriding response required from us is to trust that God is in this, and that he is actively working these things for our good, and not for evil. When we do not know what God is doing, or why, it is the time to express our confidence in him and say, "As yet, I don't know what you're up to, but I know this: you are acting for my good, and

---

[45]   Hosea 4:6

in due season you will reveal to me your wisdom." This trusting attitude will affect a positive mental and emotional response, giving confidence in the present and hope for the future. Praise and thanksgiving will well up within us instead of pity and despair.

The third signpost is learning to position ourselves rightly before God. Embrace the process; do not resist it. Desire God's outcome, bending your will to his, and submit to his timelines. When a woman is expecting the birth of a child, she is advised in breathing techniques and how to cooperate with the contractions instead of resisting them. Resistance only protracts the length and severity of labour, making the birth process more painful and difficult. Going with the flow of the Spirit enables the will of God to operate in good time with a most positive outcome.

> Set the Lord at your right hand. Therefore you will not be shaken and boundary lines set for you fall in pleasant places.[46]

The fourth signpost is learning to rest in him. The Lady Julian of Norwich said, "All shall be well, and all manner of things shall be well."[47] He is *Jehovah-shalom*, the Lord our Peace. He is our peace, and he dwells in peace. We need to practise coming into his presence and quieting ourselves before him. "Be still, and know that I am God."[48] We learn to be still in him not to empty our minds but to be filled with him. We cannot control external noise, but we can take control over our interior life. We seek to live from the inside out. We order our world by ordering our hearts. Resting in him makes us strong and confident.[49]

The fifth signpost is learning to recognise that God is more process-oriented than event-oriented. Lasting positive change takes time. God is not in a hurry, and neither should we be. He is patient and persevering. He is always on time: never too late

---

46   Psalm 16:5-6
47   Julian of Norwich, *Revelations of Divine Love*, Ch. 27. Julian of Norwich (ca. 1342-1416) wrote the earliest surviving book in the English language to be written by a woman.
48   Psalm 46:10
49   Isaiah 40:29-31

or too early. We need to learn how to respond in God's timing. The way of the Spirit operates in times and seasons. "There is a proper time and procedure for every matter."[50] We need to think process not event.

The sixth signpost is to understand that God's perfect will is habitation, not visitation. God's desire is not to have visitation rights but to be a permanent resident. He inhabits his people. Home is where God dwells, and he has made his home in us. "Christ in you, the hope of glory."[51] His language is less about visiting and more about abiding. Those who abide in Christ need no reviving. The need for revival in the Body of Christ is evidence of poor health, if not death. Christ has taken up residence within us, and his Spirit seeks to expand his territory. Our Father's loving and irrepressible passion is to grow us from spiritual babies to spiritual adults, mature with the things of Christ.

> Show me your ways. O Lord; Teach me your paths. Lead me in your truth and teach me, for you are the God of my salvation; on you I wait all the day.[52]

> Teach me your ways, O Lord, and I will walk in your truth. Give me an undivided heart that I may revere you.[53]

50	Ecclesiastes 8:6
51	Colossians 1:27
52	Psalm 25:4-5
53	Psalm 86:11

Prayer

*Lord Jesus Christ,
ever-living and ever-present,
make known to us the ways of God and his purpose for our lives.
Interpret to us the meaning of your incarnate life
and open our eyes to see you working in and among us.
Make relevant to our lives and the world in which we live the truth about yourself.
Continue your transformational work in our lives
and let us grow in apprehending your mind and heart and character.
Infuse into us your Spirit
to be our light, our life, our love, our strength.
Our ever-living and ever-present Lord,
teach us how to be one with you!*

2

The Bridegroom God

I am my beloved's, and my beloved is mine . . . He brought me to his banqueting house, and his banner over me was love . . . My beloved spoke to me, and said to me: "Rise up, my love, my fair one, and come away . . . The time of singing has come . . ." My beloved is mine, and I am his.[54]

The Bridegroom God

> He who loves Me will be loved by My Father, and I will love him and manifest Myself to him . . . If anyone loves me, he will keep My word; and My Father will love him, and We will come to him and make Our home with him.[55]

The Bible reveals there is far more trafficking between heaven and earth than we suppose. Jacob encountered God in a dream and saw a ladder, a stairway, stretching from earth to heaven, and there appeared angels ascending and descending upon it.[56] Angels are constantly engaged in a two-way flow of traffic bridging the gulf between the Throne of God and the very patch of earth we each stand on. Francis Thompson captured the wonder of heaven's commerce and correspondence in "the traffic of Jacob's ladder pitched between Heaven and Charing Cross".[57]

---

54 Song of Solomon 2:4, 10-12, 16, 6:3 NKJV
55 John 14:20-21, 23 NKJV
56 Genesis 28:12
57 "The Kingdom of God" by Francis Thompson (1859–1907)

We may be conscious of our prayers ascending Jacob's Ladder, but it can come as a surprise when we experience the downward movement from heaven to earth. God is a communicator, and he delights in interacting with humanity. His correspondence comes from a deep yearning to connect and unite in love with us.

Christianity reveals God is a lover. The Bible is his open love letter to us. He is ever seeking to court us and pursue us as the Hound of Heaven, until we become completely his. The Hebrew word for the Bible is *mikra*, which means "the calling out of God". God is calling out to us from the Scriptures, seeking to woo us and draw us to himself with cords of love.[58] He calls to us to come, know and love him just as he knows and loves us. He longs for us to let him prove himself as the extravagant lover he truly is. His abiding desire is for us to be courted and wooed by him. He wants us to grasp the truth of who he wants to be for us and know the indomitable, irrepressible and irresistible love he has for each and every one of us.

Throughout the Bible, the Lord speaks in terms of a bridegroom's desire for his bride. John the Baptist described himself as the Friend, or Bestman, of the Bridegroom-Messiah. God is represented in the Bible by many images, all of which express his jealous longing for us. Prominent among these images is the Bridegroom God. The picture is of God as a bridegroom who lavishes his love upon his chosen bride.

> As the bridegroom rejoices in his bride, so will your God rejoice in you.[59]

He wants us to recognise his deep longing to be in an intimate relationship with us. He wants us to see him as the heavenly Bridegroom and ourselves as the spiritual Bride he longs to lavish his love upon. He wants us to allow ourselves to be courted by him, so that we can grasp this mind-blowing truth and comprehend his unchanging, unconquerable, and irrepressible love for each and every one of us. His love is eternal and unconditional. It

---

58   Hosea 11:4
59   Isaiah 62:5

is not limited or conditioned by our love for him. The apostle Paul says, "While we were still sinners, Christ died for us."[60] His nature makes it impossible for him to neglect or abandon us. The blood-soaked earth at the foot of Jesus' cross is the permanent witness that God is forever committed to his love relationship with us.

We cannot wear out his welcome. It is impossible for us to do anything to make him love us any more than he already does and neither is it possible to do anything to make him love us any less. God is eternal and everything he does is everlasting. He loves with an eternal love. We have been judged to be loved for eternity. God is capable of loving us without limits. It is his nature. Our sin does not have to separate us from the love of God. Jesus came to liberate us from sin and to claim us as his spiritual Bride. His commitment to his Bride is total. He detests any suggestion of divorce.[61]

> Therefore what God has joined together, let not man separate.[62]

His covenant with his Bride is indissoluble. He is faithful "for better, for worse; for richer, for poorer; in sickness and in health" and, in his case, death shall not part him from us. He loves with a passion.

> A passion stronger than death, his ardour is as unyielding as the grave. Many waters cannot quench love, nor can the floods drown it.[63]

Our Bridegroom God would rather suffer the pain of our insults and rejections toward him than abandon us.

> How can I give you up, Ephraim? How can I hand you over, Israel? . . . My heart churns within Me; My sympathy is stirred . . . For I am God, and not a man, the Holy One in your midst, and I will not come with terror.[64]

---

60 Romans 5:8
61 Malachi 2:16
62 Mark 10:9 NKJV
63 Songs 8:6-7 NKJV
64 Hosea 11:8-9 NKJV

His love is patient and long-suffering. He is ever-hopeful, confident in his own ability to reach us and eventually win through. He thinks long distance and sets himself for a marathon, not a quick sprint. He is not pressurised by time; he has eternity on his side. Nothing escapes him. He works all things together for our good.

> Your unfailing love, O Lord, is as vast as the heavens; your faithfulness reaches beyond the clouds.[65]

The Bride Price and the Wedding Garments

On the night Jesus was betrayed, at the Lord's Supper, he gave his disciples the familiar Passover bread and cup of thanksgiving, and blessed them with a new significance. Jesus said, "This is My body . . . My . . . blood."[66] In effect, he was saying, "Eat, drink. I am offering you my life." In those days, a Jewish bridegroom would make a proposal of marriage by negotiating a bride price and seek the bride's approval of the arrangement by offering a cup of wine and handing it to her. This gesture meant: "I am offering my life to you". If the bride was willing to marry him, she took the cup and drank from it. Her action signified, "I receive your life, and I give you mine in return." Then the wedding ceremony would proceed.

At the Last Supper, when Jesus handed the cup of wine to his disciples, he was virtually saying, "Will you marry me? Will you be my spiritual bride?" His followers had a decision to make. To drink from his cup signified accepting Jesus' marriage proposal, receiving his life and offering theirs in return.

At a Jewish wedding, two arrangements had to be taken care of in order to make good the bridegroom's proposal: the payment of the bride price and the provision of wedding garments for the guests. Our Bridegroom God has taken care of both necessary wedding arrangements. Jesus' love for us compelled him to do whatever it took to pay for his chosen Bride. He paid for all of us, for all eternity. The bride price was exorbitant, beyond

---

65 Psalm 35 NIV
66 Luke 22:19-20

calculation, beyond anything we could afford. It cost Jesus everything. It cost him his life, and yet he paid the price willingly.

> Father, if it is possible, let this cup of suffering be taken from me. Yet not what I want, but what you want![67]

Drinking from the communion cup is not simply taking a sip of wine, but a symbol of Jesus' marriage proposal and our willingness to embrace our identity as his spiritual bride.

To celebrate the union of the groom and bride, wedding garments were offered to the guests at the wedding banquet. To refuse such an offer would have been deeply offensive. Jesus' Parable of the Wedding Garments signified that at the wedding feast of the Lamb we cannot wear just anything.[68] We have to be properly dressed. We cannot be clothed in our own righteousness; it is not good enough. When Jesus paid the price for our sins on the cross, he accomplished our salvation and made us right with God. We must put on the gift of righteousness Christ purchased for us to wear.

No matter how unworthy we may feel, we are totally accepted in Christ. God's extravagant love and unconditional acceptance of us is not based on our goodness or lack of it; it is based on Christ's goodness—on the bride price he paid for us. We now carry the unearned privilege of being his beloved Bride. Jesus has betrothed us to himself forever.

> I am my Beloved's, and he is mine, and his banner over me is love.[69]

> *Love bade me welcome: yet my soul drew back,*
> *guilty of dust and sin.*
> *But quick-eyed Love, observing me grow slack*
> *from my first entrance in,*
> *drew nearer to me, sweetly questioning,*
> *if I lacked anything.*
> *A guest, I answered, worthy to be here.*
> *Love said, You shall be he.*

---

67 Matthew 26:29
68 Matthew 22:2-3, 10-14
69 Song of Solomon 2:4

> *I the unkind, ungrateful? Ah, my dear,*
> *I cannot look on thee.*
> *Love took my hand, and smiling did reply,*
> *Who made the eyes but I?*
> *Truth Lord, but I have marred them: let my shame*
> *go where it doth deserve.*
> *And know you not, says Love, who bore the blame?*
> *My dear, then I will serve.*
> *You must sit down, says Love, and taste my meat.*
> *So I did sit and eat.*[70]

Jesus says in the Book of Revelation, "Behold, I stand at the door and knock. If anyone hears My voice and opens the door, I will come in to him and dine with him, and he with Me."[71]

The First Cause

There was nothing exceptional about the boy in the opening story. He was, and still is, fallible, as prone to character weakness as anyone else. His experience was not a reward for good behaviour, and he did not become an exceptional, world-renowned hero of the Christian faith in his adult life. His encounter with God was unearned and undeserved. It was simply due to the extraordinary, undeserved grace of God reaching from heaven to an inexperienced, immature boy, who was seeking Jesus. Christ initiated the encounter. He made the first move. He is the First and Prime Mover with all of us. It was the Lord's choice to meet with the boy in that way. Yet this story contains a universal truth applicable to all lovers of Christ.

Jesus said to his followers,

> At that day you will know that I am in the Father, and you in Me, and I in you. He who has My commands and keeps them, it is he who loves Me. And he who loves Me will be loved by My Father, and I will love him and manifest Myself to him . . . If anyone loves me, he will keep My word; and My Father will love him, and We will come to him and make Our home with him.[72]

70	George Herbert, "Love Bade Me Welcome", a 17th century poem
71	Revelation 3:20
72	John 14:20-21, 23

All Christ's followers, without distinction, are loved by him. The Lord has no favourites. We are all saved by grace through the blood of Christ and his completed work on the cross. Each one of us is accepted by the Father in the Beloved, Jesus Christ. His acceptance of us is complete, total. He accepts us, not in part, but nothing less than one hundred percent. We cannot improve on that. There is no room for adding to what Jesus has done for us. We cannot get God to love us or accept us more than he already does. His acceptance of us is not a Good Conduct Medal. Just as we are, we are totally and wonderfully accepted in the Beloved.

The Father said of his Son Jesus, "This is My beloved Son, in whom I am well pleased."[73] The moment we accepted Christ into our lives, the Spirit of Jesus entered us and took up residence within us. The Father sees Jesus in us, and he responds to us as he would to Jesus, with the same words, "This is my beloved son, daughter, in whom I am well pleased." We become the *be-loved* of God, totally accepted, for all eternity, with the promise "I will never leave you nor forsake you."

Lover and the Be-loved

He is the Lover and we are the be-loved.[74] He has set his affection upon us. It was his choice and his initiative. As the be-loved, our first call is to allow ourselves to be loved by God. What is the Christian's first calling? Contrary to popular belief, it is not to love God. That is our second calling. Our first calling is to allow God to love us. Our relationship with God is not primarily founded upon our love for him but on his love for us. God first loved us, while we were yet sinners, while we had done nothing to deserve his attention or affection. He is the Prime Mover in the relationship. He is the Alpha to our lives. It is his job to be the Lover, and it is our job to be the be-loved. To be the be-loved, we need to open ourselves up to be loved by him. Then by receiving his love, we can return his love to him and to others.

---

73   Matthew 3:17
74   1 John 3:2

We can love God only if we have first learned to receive his love for us. We cannot give what we do not have. First, we must learn to let ourselves be loved by God, and then we can respond by returning his love. The be-loved must learn to be loved. Not forgetting our "first love" is a cause we will need to return to again and again in our lives.[75]

We can so easily be distracted and go off track in our discipleship when we forget to practise this first love. Ezekiel saw a vision about a river that flowed from the Temple,[76] and in a similar way the flow of God's love within us gets increasingly deeper and wider when we allow ourselves to be loved by God. Constantly practising the presence of God and bathing in his love for us will save us from spiritual sterility and aridity and help us avoid the bankruptcy of a heartless Christianity. We can sow only what we reap.

Grace Clouds

Nature abhors a vacuum. Wherever there is emptiness, other forces will seek to rush in and fill the space. Our topmost priority in the spiritual life is to focus on God's immense and indomitable love for us. Then, and only then, should our second priority be to focus on our love for God. To maintain our conscious awareness of being the be-loved, we must practise being loved in our devotional lives. We need to develop a high view of God's sovereign grace and majestic mercy. We need to absorb the written Word of Truth, where it speaks of the love of Christ for us. We need to dig increasingly deeper into the infinite height, depth and breadth of Christ's love for us. For every mountain of difficulty in our lives, Christ's love is higher still. For every deep pit of sin, Christ's love is deeper still to rescue us. No matter how wide an obstacle in our lives, Christ's love is wider still to cover us. No matter how long temptation lasts, Christ's love is long enough to last a lifetime and beyond into eternity. Underneath us are the everlasting arms. His love covers a multitude of sins.

---

75   Revelation 2:4
76   Ezekiel 47:1-2

As far as the east is from the west, so far has he cast our sins from us. Nothing can separate us from the love of God that is in Christ Jesus. We are loved with an everlasting love, and God has no favourites. He does not prefer one son over another. All his children are under grace.

Think of God's grace being like rain. The rain does not discriminate between people; it pours on all of us alike. Imagine that wherever we go, we are constantly under a cloud, a cloud of his presence. Remember that Jesus says, "I am with you always."[77] There is an *always* to the presence of God with us. Imagine that this cloud of grace is not a dry cloud, but it rains down blessing and unearned favour upon us all the time. We live under an open heaven. God's delight is to soak us continually with his grace. There is a way to prevent ourselves from getting wet: put up an umbrella. Under an umbrella, we are hiding under a false covering. The umbrella does not cause the rain to stop; it simply prevents the rain from reaching the person underneath. Under the umbrella he is dry, without grace, even though grace is continuing to fall all over and around him. Disobedience and self-reliance create umbrellas in people's lives, yet God's grace is still available to them. Such is the miracle the cross of Christ has accomplished for us!

Because of Jesus' finished work on the cross for us, we have been adopted and totally accepted by God. On our good days, we are loved, accepted and approved. On our bad days, though our behaviour is not approved of by God, yet we are still accepted, because we are "in Christ".[78] Recognition of such undeserved and unconditional love would melt the hardness of our hearts and cause any Bride of Christ to turn back to him and seek reformation and restoration in the embrace of the Bridegroom God.[79]

---

77   Matthew 28:20
78   Ephesians 1:7
79   Revelation 19:7-8

The Song of the Beloved

Place me like a seal over your heart,
like a seal on your arm;
for love is as strong as death,
its jealousy[80] unyielding as the grave.
It burns like blazing fire,
like a mighty flame.
Many waters cannot quench love;
rivers cannot sweep it away.
If one were to give
all the wealth of one's house for love,
it would be utterly scorned.[81]

---

80   Ardour, passion, fervour, zeal
81   Song of Solomon 8:6-7 ESV

A Prayer

I come to you, Lord Jesus Christ,
my passionate Bridegroom,
knowing that your delight is for me.
I know that you have invited me to come and search you out
and that you will never ever turn me away.
I can never get too close to you.
The further and more intensely I seek after you,
even as a bride would seek to obtain the affections of
and to show her affections toward
her bridegroom,
the more you reveal yourself to me.
There is no end to the affections of your heart.
The desire of your heart toward me is an unquenchable ocean
ready for me to dive deeply into—
as deeply as I would ever want.
Even judgments that are directly from your hand
are the products of your desire
to obtain love from the hearts of your human bride.
You will allow nothing to stand between your heart
and the objects of your affection.
Your zeal will remove everything
that hinders love from being received by me.
You come back, again and again, to simply love me.
Everything in my life works out for my own benefit
because it is you who loves me
and works to form complete and mature love in my heart,
love for you and love for other people.
Set my heart on fire with the unquenchable fire that
resides deep inside of you, Jesus. Amen.

3

Called by Love

Nothing happens unless first we dream.[82]

I've always said that one night, I'm going to find myself in a field somewhere, I'm standing on grass, and it's raining, and I'm with the person I love, and I know I'm at the very point I've been dreaming of getting to.[83]

A Night-time Visitation

The boy was startled from his deep sleep by a loud crash of thunder shaking the night sky. His small, darkened room was heavy with the unseen but palpable presence of God. Another flash of lightning followed. A voice called his name. Barely awake, and hardly aware of what he was saying, words tumbled from his mouth, "Yes, Lord. I'm listening." A voice came, "Be still. Do not be afraid. I am with you."

He hid the experience in his heart for some years, refusing to share it with others. His parents were not obvious believers and had not been church attenders. Religious belief was not a subject discussed in the home. They were not opposed to Christianity; they were merely indifferent. Even so, the boy had been conscious of the Lord's presence from his earliest years. He had a natural, simplistic belief in the existence of God and his love. Looking at star-filled skies, he would marvel at the greatness and majesty of

---
82   Carl Sandburg, American Pulitzer prize-winning poet, 1878-1967
83   Drew Barrymore, American actress

God. He always believed that God was close, loving, and big. From childhood, he would experience comforting times of falling asleep at night with the satisfaction of sensing Jesus holding his outstretched hand.

There were special visitations when the Lord's presence would fire and excite his heart, leaving him in awe. Then there were unusual times when the presence of the Lord was so strong that it left him overwhelmed.

A True Calling Has a Caller

From the very beginnings of human history, God has been calling out to his people. He is a calling God. Scripture frequently refers to God as one who calls out to people. The Bible is a record of his dealings and reveals how he is constantly calling out. His constant pursuit of us is motivated by his abiding desire to draw us to himself. "We are not called primarily to do something or go somewhere; we are called to Someone",[84] to an intimate, affectionate relationship with God our "First Love".[85] God draws us to himself so that everything we are and all that we do, the whole of our lives, lives in response to his call.

The word "church" is translated from the Greek *ekklesia*, whose root meaning is "called out", and its Old Testament Hebrew equivalent *qahal* carries the idea of "a called out people". The word "vocation" is synonymous with calling. It comes from the Latin root words *voca* meaning "to call", *vox* meaning "voice", and *vocatio* meaning "to call, summon". All of this clarifies our understanding that a true vocation has something to do with a voice. It is vocalised, produced by a voice. It is evident, then, that the Christian's vocation is a calling, spoken out and issued by the voice of a Caller. There can be no true calling without a caller. "If there is no Caller, there are no callings—only work."[86] For Christians, this calling is from God. Every Christian is called by God. The Christian's vocation is not the same as his or her

---

84 Os Guinness, *The Call*, 43
85 Revelation 2:4
86 Os Guinness, *The Call*, 42

career or profession, yet there is an overlap between a vocation and a profession. There is a common misunderstanding where vocation is thought of as a call to do, yet it is important to understand that our primary call from God is to be. We are called by Love to be loved and to love. It is helpful to think of vocation in two ways: *primary* and *secondary*. Our primary vocation is to a relationship with God himself, as a follower of Christ. Our secondary calling is the activities we are called to perform with nothing too mundane or secular.

> *Teach me, my God and King,*
> *In all things Thee to see,*
> *And what I do in anything*
> *To do it as for Thee.*
> *A man that looks on glass,*
> *On it may stay his eye;*
> *Or if he pleaseth, through it pass,*
> *And then the heaven espy.*[87]

Face to Face

The Lord God called out to Adam, "Where are you?"[88] A father was looking for his son.[89] The story pictures God taking a stroll in the Garden in the cool of the day. It was his daily pleasure to have downtime with Adam when the day's work had finished. Adam could relax and enjoy his friendship with his Creator and Father. It is a beautiful picture of intimacy between the Creator and the creatures he had made in his image. In the beginning they had enjoyed openness, harmony and joy together. "Where are you?" is the call of a pained father to a missing son and daughter, but we need to remember that this is the call of an omniscient, omnipresent, and omnipotent God. God is all-knowing. All hearts are open to him and no secrets are hidden from him. He says, "My eyes are on all their ways. They are not hidden from me."[90] His vision is better than Superman's

---

87   George Herbert, hymn "Teach me, my God and King", 1633
88   Genesis 3:9
89   Luke 3:38
90   Jeremiah 16:17

X-ray vision. God knew the exact location of Adam and Eve's hiding place.[91] We are never out of sight from God. The Lord was not asking a question of geography, a physical place, but of relationship. His question was a heart issue. "Adam, Eve, where are you now in your hearts with me? Where are you in relation to me?"

The all-knowing God did not need to ask the question for his own sake but for theirs. He questions us in order that we would question ourselves and recognise the reality of our current position. "*Where* are you? *Who* have you been listening to? *Have* you turned from my ways? *What* is it you have done?"[92] Notice that not once did Adam and Eve offer an apology. We might wonder how things would have turned out if they had! God's question of Adam and Eve is pertinent for all of us. "Where are you now in relation to me?" God made us for himself that we would enjoy him and live in close friendship with him for ever. His question "Where are you?" focuses on our vocation to be loved by God and to enjoy loving him.[93]

God's creation of Adam was special and unique. He made Adam not only from the clay of the earth but he breathed his own Spirit into him. William Blake, the poet and mystic, gave a fascinating picture of the Creator God stretched out upon Adam's lifeless body, breathing his Spirit into him mouth to mouth. It is not the act of a distant God but one who came up close and personal. It is an act of real intimacy. We can imagine that as God bent close to breathe into Adam's mouth and nostrils, he looked directly into Adam's face, watching for the first sign of life when Adam would open his eyes for the first time. As Adam opened his eyes, the very first thing he would see was the face of God smiling at him, full of delight and love for his "son". In that moment, the first thing God would see was a reflection of his own image smiling back at him; son like Father.

---

91   Psalm 139:9-13
92   Genesis 3:9-13
93   Westminster Shorter Catechism says, "The chief end of man is to glorify God and to enjoy him for ever."

The Lord make his face shine upon you and be gracious to you; the Lord turn his face toward you and give you peace.[94]

Adam and Eve's falling away broke that communion yet all was not lost. The eternal Father had a plan. Christ came as the Second Adam to repair the breach and restore humanity to the destiny God had planned from the beginning. All those who abide in Christ are seen and received by the Father as bearing Christ's likeness. He sees Christ "in us". He sees beyond the clay to the treasure within. He looks into the eyes of our hearts and sees the image of his Son looking back at him. "This is my beloved son, daughter, in whom I am well pleased. These are my beloved children in whom I delight." God made and redeemed each one of us for his pleasure and delight.[95]

Our vocation is, first and foremost, a call to know and be loved by God. We are called to be his friends. It is primarily a call to become rather than a call to do. When God called, "Where are you?" it was not a call to a park attendant, an employee, a functionary. It was not a call to something or somewhere, but a call to Someone. He called us for ourselves. He calls each one of us by name, individually and personally.

The Call to Become

The call of God addresses us by name as unique individuals, precious, significant, and free to respond to his invitation to be drawn into a personal friendship with him. He says, "I have called you by name."[96] Our freedom means that our future is not unchangeably carved in stone. We do not choose our destiny. We either fulfil it or fail it. We are not the puppets of some predetermined fate, but being human means we have the freedom to respond or not to God's call to us in Christ. Following God's call leads us forward. We become what we are not yet.

---

94 Numbers 6:25-26 NIV
95 Ephesians 1:5
96 Isaiah 43:1

Human identity is neither fixed nor final in this life. It is incomplete.[97]

The call of God is to Christ, the Omega, the Ultimate, to full human existence. Each person's destiny and future becoming rests with Christ. Those who refuse to respond to his call forfeit the final transformation and trans-signification of their being. Those who respond to his call will rise to become the glorious beings he calls us to be. We become our real selves when we respond to Christ and follow his call. We are beings in the process of becoming.

> My lover spoke and said to me, "Arise, my darling, my beautiful one, and come with me."[98]

The call of God will change our perspectives: how we view ourselves and others. Jesus asked a question of the Pharisees who despised the woman who washed Jesus' feet with her tears as their spiritual inferior. "Do you see this woman?"[99] In effect he was asking, "Do you see the real person here? Do you see her as God sees her? Do you see her for herself and not simply the wrongs she has committed? Beyond the mire and clay, can you see the treasure within?" Because she had experienced God's extravagant, forgiving love, she was filled with love and gratitude toward God. Jesus saw the love of God within her. Love recognises its existence in others. It treasures the mutuality of its own existence.

We go seriously wrong when we lose sight of others' unique worth in the eyes of God. There is a danger of seeing them as mere functionaries for our personal ambitions, a means to an end, with a shelf life, in our pursuit for career success. Christian ministry, at any level, is not immune from this. Evangelists can view converts as numbers notched up on their gun belt with no real interest in their further development as disciples. "Successful" church leaders can treat those they are responsible for as mere

---

97   Os Guinness, *The Call*, 24
98   Song of Songs 2:10
99   Luke 7:44-47

objects to serve their own empire-building. It is so important to watch what the office does to the office-holder and not merely what the office-holder does to the office. God's will carried out in any way but God's way is not God's will. The measure of a person is how he uses the power given him. When God measures the greatness of a person, he puts the tape measure around his heart, not his head.

The call of Jesus to his followers is a personal invitation to centre their lives on him. It requires our willingness to allow him to lead us in the way he wants us to go, to identify ourselves with him and to act in his name. But before interpreting this as a call to service, it is first and foremost a call to worship, to live in close fellowship with him, and make him the model for shaping our identity. Before all else, the call "Come, follow me" is a call to make Jesus "the great heart of our own heart".[100] Ever before Jesus sent out his disciples to teach and preach, the gospel says he called them to be "with him".[101] The priority is companionship, relationship-building by close proximity, like osmosis!

He calls us to be, to turn our lives around and surrender our hearts and minds to become like him. He calls us to be mirror-images of himself and to reflect his life and nature to others. Again, we see God's call is primarily one of relationship, to be, and only secondly, to do. He comes to each believer to live within them by the power of his Spirit[102] and, like the action of yeast, it is his constant permeating work within us. He lives from our inside out.

The call of God will change how we see ourselves and how we see others. We see ourselves and others as Christ the Bridegroom sees his Bride: "My darling, my beautiful one". Our beauty does not come from ourselves but from Christ's undeserved presence within us, "love to the loveless shown, that they might lovely be."

---

100   From the hymn "Be Thou My Vision", a hymn based on 6th century Irish hymn and translated by Eleanor Hull and published in 1912.
101   Mark 3:13-14
102   1 John 4:15

The Most Compelling Adventure

My song is love unknown,
My Saviour's love to me;
Love to the loveless shown,
That they might lovely be.[103]

The trees in Eden, which were intended as the context for man's freedom and delight in a close relationship with God,[104] became the context of a cover up. Adam hid from the presence of God. Yet another tree, the tree of Calvary, calls us to rise to an elevated life with Christ in the heavenly places.[105]

God's unchanging quest is to raise many sons and daughters to glory,[106] to an exalted state of eternal existence in his presence, overcoming all barriers to his indomitable and irrepressible love through the redeeming blood of Christ.

When I am lifted up I will draw all people to myself.[107]

We were made by divine love for divine love. Love is his meaning. God's call beckons us to plunge ourselves into his own divine likeness.

Come and enter your Master's happiness.[108]

It is the way of God to call out, to beckon. Every Christian is called by God. God calls out to us through the Scriptures and various other ways. Some will perceive the call of God as an inward whisper warming their hearts and drawing them to himself. Others will perceive the stirrings of God in their soul through their intellectual quest, while others will need their attention woken and their disabling self-doubts overcome by more dramatic and sensational means.

Although our ultimate authority is Scripture, there are other modes of calling, and one is not superior to another, whether the

---

103   Samuel Crossman, hymn "My Song is Love Unknown", 1664
104   "You may *freely eat*"—Genesis 2:16
105   Ephesians 2:6
106   Hebrews 2:10
107   John 12:32
108   Matthew 25:21

call is perceived through visual and audible external phenomena or by internal impressions. What counts is not the means by which we receive God's calls but the fruit produced from heeding them, by whatever means they come.

In fact, an external manifestation carries its own temptations. People can become unhealthily dependent on such manifestations and find it problematic to rest their faith on God's word from Scripture. They can become over-dependent upon sensations and feelings rather than faith alone making them highly vulnerable in times of aridity and wilderness seasons scheduled by the Spirit. The Lord often needs to wean such people from a too strong attachment to sensations and soulish spirituality. Hence, the way of the Spirit is to liberate through times of aridity and purging of the senses and lead the believer to greater maturity in his walk with God.

God calls out to each and every one of us. In love he bids us welcome just as we are. His love desires to mould and shape us into vessels of honour and put his treasure within. With cords of kindness and ties of love he seeks to draw us into the direction of his will.[109] As a 14th century Christian writer said,

> For he can well be loved, but he cannot be thought. By love he can be grasped and held, but by thought, neither grasped nor held.[110]

C.S. Lewis wrote,

> We do not want merely to see beauty, though, God knows, even that is bounty enough. We want something else which can hardly be put into words—to be united with the beauty we see, to pass into it, to receive it into ourselves, to bathe in it, to become part of it.[111]

---

109   Hosea 11:4
110   *The Cloud of Unknowing*, an anonymous Christian work written in the latter half of the 14th century as a spiritual guide on contemplative prayer, reputedly inspired generations of spiritual directors such as John of the Cross and Pierre Teilhard de Chardin. Prior to this, the theme of the cloud had appeared in *The Confessions of St. Augustine* (IX, 10) written in AD 398.
111   C.S. Lewis, *The Weight of Glory*, 42

We were made for beauty, for the source of beauty, for God himself.

Prayer

*My Lord Jesus, let me follow you
in simplicity and faith.
Be such a part of my life that my attitudes,
my thinking and behaviour will be built on you.
May I know you so intimately that I may speak of you
naturally and happily.
Help me to be your follower in every part of my life
and in every day of my life,
that walking in the ways you have prepared for me,
I may find my life in doing your will.*

4

Responding to the Caller

Alack, thou knowest not
how little worthy of any love thou art!
Whom wilt thou find to love ignoble thee
save Me, save only Me?
All which I took from thee I did but take,
not for thy harms.
But just that thou might'st seek it in my arms.
All which thy child's mistake
fancies as lost, I have stored for thee at home;
Rise, clasp My hand, and come![112]

From Ordinary to Significant

A sense of being called by the Lord had been growing in the boy over some years. His desire for Christ increased with a growing sense of personal commitment and, at sixteen years of age, he took himself to church and shortly made a public commitment to Christ.

There was one issue that troubled him: his sense of feeling unworthy. He offered himself to serve in many ways in his local church. He was just an average teenager, with the usual insecurities and struggles. He came from working-class parents, was raised on a council estate, with little experience of the world. His self-doubt and sense of unworthiness gnawed at him, making

---

112   Francis Thompson, "The Hound of Heaven", 1893

him believe that his inexperience and immaturity must surely count against him. He felt he did not measure up as a candidate for ordained ministry and yet the sense of calling pursued him like a hound of heaven.

In an unguarded moment, he shared with his Minister his sense of vocation, not expecting anything much to happen. To his utter surprise, he received a call from the Bishop's office asking to meet and discuss his calling. He was only eighteen.

Two years later, and after much scrutiny, he would be accepted for ordination training. Who could have guessed that, although questioning himself on his suitability and ability, he would spend the next fifty years of his life ministering and training thousands of believers not only in his own country but in many countries throughout the world? He certainly did not! Yet this is precisely what can happen when shapeless, wet clay yields to the fashioning hands of the all-wise and loving Master Potter.

> Brothers, think of what you were when you were called. Not many of you were wise by human standards; not many were influential; not many were of noble birth. But God chose the foolish things of the world to shame the wise; God chose the weak things of the world to shame the strong. He chose the lowly things of the world and the despised things—and the things that are not—to nullify the things that are, so that no one may boast before him.[113]

> When they saw the courage of Peter and John and realized that they were unschooled, ordinary men, they were astonished and they took note that these men had been with Jesus.[114]

The greatest challenges to our calling are fear and poor self-worth. Unworthiness can come from one of two sources: poor self-image or a genuine appreciation of unmerited, undeserved privilege. The Bible tells us that true love casts out all fear.[115] We overcome fear with more love.

---

113   1 Corinthians 1:26-29 NIV
114   Acts 4:13 NIV
115   1 John 4:18

Anyone who studies God's ways soon realises they are quite different from man's ways.[116] His ways are far superior in wisdom and love. Worldly wisdom tells us that extraordinary people and abundant resources are needed for great tasks, yet the Lord often chooses the small and insignificant to achieve his purposes on earth.

Christ selected a rather ordinary group of men as his disciples, yet after being filled with the Spirit, they turned the world upside down. During his ministry on earth, Jesus fed thousands with a child's meagre lunch, and he viewed the widow's two small coins as a greater offering than all the larger amounts given.

To accomplish his tasks, God specialises in using people who are not naturally qualified. Moses was a verbally impaired 80-year-old shepherd who liberated a nation. After Gideon hid from the enemy, God made him a mighty warrior. David was the overlooked youngest son, yet he killed a giant with a small stone and became Israel's king and a man after God's own heart.

The Lord is not looking for impressive people. He wants willing ones, who will bow the knee in humble submission. Being weak and ordinary does not make us useless. Rather, it positions us for a demonstration of divine power in our lives. God delights in using our dependence to display his glory.

Have we considered that our lack of ability, talent, or skill could be the ideal setting for a great display of Christ's power and glory? If we are willing to submit to his leading and venture into the scary yet rewarding territory of faith and obedience, he will do great things in and through us. We will journey in the most compelling adventure of all.

"Follow Me"

God calls his friends. If being called by God is an act of friendship on his part, then accepting his call is an act of friendship on our part. As Jesus said, "You are my friends if you do what I command. I no longer call you servants."[117]

---

116   Isaiah 55:8-9
117   John 15:14-15 NIV

Throughout the Bible we see God calling all sorts of people in all sorts of ways. "Many are called!"[118] Jesus called the twelve, then the seventy-two, and eventually his call extends to all believers in every time and place.[119] His words are simple and unequivocal, "Come, follow me."[120] The New Testament Greek word for "follow" is *akdoutheo*, which expresses the notion of union, likeness, and comes from a root word meaning "one going in the same way". To follow Christ is to go the same way as he did—discipleship. Jesus says, "I am the way".[121] A Christian disciple is the one who seeks to imitate Christ in all that he was and all that he did. It is a call to resemble him and walk in his ways. It is to identify with him so closely that we find ourselves being transformed into his likeness. It has the further meaning of representation: we are call to represent his presence and life. The way of God is to send us out to do the same things Jesus was doing.

The word "submission" (sub-mission) means to be under or serve another's mission. Jesus was under the mission of his Father, and we are called to be under the mission of Christ.

There is a saying in the Jewish world: to be covered in the dust of your rabbi. It describes the especially close bond to be enjoyed between a rabbi and his disciple. The chosen disciple would walk so closely upon the heels of his rabbi that he would be covered in his road dust. The disciple would yearn to learn everything he could from his teacher, not only hearing every word but imitating his every action and the manner of his life. His purpose was to become completely like his master in word and action; whatever his master said, he said, and whatever his master did, he did. It was the implication behind Jesus' words to his disciples at the feeding of the five thousand, when he said to them, "You feed them!"[122] This was the same implication behind Peter's words to Jesus, when he said to him, "Tell me to come

---

118	Matthew 22:14
119	Matthew 28:19-20
120	Matthew 4:19
121	John 14:6
122	Mark 6:37 NLT

to you on the water!", and Jesus' response was "Come!"[123] Peter understood that if he was "covered in the dust of his rabbi" he was meant to be and do everything his Master was and did.

Only when we respond to Christ and follow his call, we become our real selves. Our calling from God is the most comprehensive reorientation and the most profound motivation in our lives. The basic question to all human existence is "Why do we exist?" The call of God is the way to finding and fulfilling the central purpose of our lives.

Can others say of us that when they encounter us they encounter God?

In Mark 3:15 Jesus calls his disciples to be in a relationship with him—that is our primary call. From this relationship, he sent them to go and do what he was doing—that is our secondary call. All Christians receive both these callings. Firstly, we are to be in a relationship with him, and from there to represent his presence and life to the world, advancing his kingdom and righteousness on earth as it is in heaven.

> We do not want merely to see beauty, though, God knows, even that is bounty enough. We want something else which can hardly be put into words—to be united with the beauty we see, to pass into it, to receive it into ourselves, to bathe in it, *to become part of it.*[124]

Calling Requires Response

Love calls to love. God desires friendship, not slavish obedience. Friendship is built on freedom of choice. God never forces his loving will on any one of us. He is not a rapist. When the angel Gabriel approached Mary with the offer of conceiving the Son of God, God respected her freedom to choose. He required Mary's yes. She could have said no. She conceived only after she responded, "Behold, the handmaid of the Lord. Be done to me according to your word."[125] She is blessed among all women because she said yes.

---

123   Matthew 14:16, 28-29
124   CS Lewis, *The Weight of Glory*, 42
125   Luke 1:38

The interaction between God and Mary is indicative of any divine vocation. When God calls, he requires a response from us. Nothing is automatic. Anything that is forced is a violation against friendship and God's own nature. Our friendship with God is so valuable to him that he allows us space to accept or reject his offer.

Almost all God's promises are conditional upon our responses. Positive responses will produce positive results. Negative responses will produce negative results. Both types of response have significant consequences. Conditional upon our responses, God's promises and callings can be fulfilled, postponed, or even cancelled altogether. King Saul's disobedience led to the cancellation of God's promise to him and his lineage.[126] Israel's rebellion at the return of the twelve spies resulted in God's promise to inherit the Promised Land to be cancelled for nearly two million people. Because of Joshua and Caleb's faithfulness, the promise of God was fulfilled for them.[127]

On the other hand, positive responses to God's call brought his favour and even a reversal of judgment. God sent Jonah to the city of Nineveh with a message of doom: "40 days and Nineveh will be overthrown."[128] But because the people listened and repented, God changed their destiny.

When God saw what they did and how they turned from their evil ways, He had compassion and did not bring upon them the destruction he had threatened.[129]

As Jesus said, "Many are called, few are chosen."[130]

> Azariah went out to meet Asa and said to him: Listen to me, Asa and all Judah and Benjamin, the Lord is with you when you are with him. If you seek him, he will be found by you, but if you forsake him, he will forsake you."[131]

126	1 Kings 13
127	Numbers 14
128	Jonah 3:4
129	Jonah 3:4, 10
130	Matthew 22:14
131	2 Chronicles 15:2

God does not circumnavigate human free will and the choices we make. He requires our cooperation. When he receives our cooperation, the prophecy then carries the power to accomplish itself: "Be it done to you according to your faith."[132]

Selective Listening: the Sower and the Seed

When Jesus listed the different responses to the seed, which is the Word of God, three responses were negative and one was positive. All three negative responses resulted in failure to see the fulfilment of God's promises. The first example depicts people who reject the Word of God outright. The second fail to see the fruition of God's Word in their lives because of shallowness. The third category of people are those who entertain God's Word for a time but allow other priorities and challenges to take over their lives and strangle God's call from their lives. Selective listening and selective interpretation affect the success of God's call in a person's life.

Jesus enunciated the principle that there is no such thing as untested faith. The success of God's callings is not automatic. It is dependent upon our responses. If it is true that a calling requires a caller, then it is equally true that the caller requires a response. It is only through reciprocated friendship that the callings of God can be activated. Love will always find a way.

Raising a Submarine

At the beginning of the twentieth century, a dangerous mission was undertaken to raise a sunken submarine from deep and dangerous waters. A young and inexperienced American naval lieutenant was put in charge of operations. It was dangerous business, far more than it is today, and the young lieutenant felt keenly his lack of expertise. The work continued for a number of weeks without success. During a time of furlough, instead of taking a break and spending the time to relax, this young naval officer used the time to train as a diver and increase his experience so as not to be such a risk to his men. Later, when the work

---

132   Matthew 9:29

of raising the submarine continued, the young officer, instead of directing operations from the safety of the ship's bridge, went over the side and risked his life with his men in the turbulent waters below. Eventually, the submarine was successfully raised, and when it was time to leave, the whole diving crew assembled on deck to say goodbye to this young officer. One man, acting for all of them, stepped forward to thank the officer, and said, "Sir, there isn't a man here who wouldn't willingly do anything in the world for you."

Doesn't this story closely parallel what Jesus did for all of us? He came on a rescue mission with the sole objective to save us and raise us to a new life with God. He willingly stepped down from the safety of his home in heaven, and, he did not just risk his life, but he gave his life for us all. Like those divers, our proper response to Jesus' call should be, "Lord, there isn't anything in the world I wouldn't willingly do for you."

Prayer

Lord Jesus, whose service is perfect freedom,
you have taught us that
we are truly free when we yield our wills to the will of the Father,
grant us that freedom of the Holy Spirit
which will not fear to tread in unknown ways
nor be held back by misgivings of ourselves
or fear of others.
Call us forward to the place of your will
which is also the place of your power.

5

The School of the Spirit

Friendship with God is a lifelong adventure. Every adventure in life has something to teach us. Every journey is instructional. Travelling brings new perspectives, fresh experiences, and we are changed by the appreciation of different cultures and the company of fellow travellers. Travelling broadens the mind. Life is a school and we travel through it having never passed this way before.

Peasants Learning to Be Princes

A German zoo, internationally known for its beautiful surroundings and animal welfare, purchased an adult brown bear from a travelling circus. It had been badly abused. For most of its life it had been imprisoned in a cage about twelve feet long. It was a miserable existence. It would spend every day, head swaying from side to side, taking twelve steps forward and twelve steps backward in its narrow prison. It was fed on stagnant water and rotten food. Because of cruelty, it walked with a limp. After purchasing the bear, the zoo released it from its cage, relocating it in beautiful parkland with the companionship of other bears. It had lush grass to walk on and trees to climb. It had fresh water to drink and was given three meals a day. Instead of enjoying its new freedom and companionship, the bear continued its pacing, twelve steps forward and twelve steps backward, head swaying from side to side, as if it was still in its cage. The zookeepers realised that the bear was not in a metal prison but in a mental prison. The prison around it was invisible and they could do nothing to free him. The kindest act was to put it to sleep.

Believers can experience a similar dilemma, when, having become accustomed to a mental trap of certain negative thought patterns, they convince themselves that things cannot change. Consequently, they are unable to enjoy the freedom and fellowship which is theirs in Christ. Facing significant mountains in their lives, they become weary and settle for far less than the Lord intended for them. Paul says,

> Be transformed by the renewing of your mind, then you will be able to test and approve God's good, pleasing, and perfect will.[133]

The work of the Holy Spirit is not finished when we are saved. He continues to work within us to transform our characters into the wholesome likeness of Christ. It is the work of sanctification. After Christ raised his friend, Lazarus, from the dead, he called him out of his tomb environment and commanded him to be released from his grave clothes. Salvation liberates us from our sin prisons, but the work of changing the programming of our past thought-patterns needs to be addressed on a daily basis. It is called "the School of the Holy Spirit".

The making of disciples requires a lifelong process of preparation. We are peasants learning to be princes.

My Father is the Gardener

Jesus employed a gardening analogy to describe God's continuous work of transforming our lives.[134] In his book *Down To Earth* the gardening presenter Monty Don writes,

> Every action has a reaction. In gardening, if you get the planting right to start with, without trying to trick a plant to behave quicker, bigger

---

133 Romans 12:2
134 John 15

or for longer, it will grow healthily and well . . . Everything you see above ground—your entire garden—is determined by what happens below ground level. All your efforts and skills should go into creating a really good root system and that will inevitably produce good foliage, flowers and fruit . . . Know and go with the seasons. Right plant, right place, right time . . . Grow for health. Timeliness is everything. Do not fight them—you will lose. Learn to be flexible and adapt. Do not accept any existing ugliness as fixed. Remove and change it if possible.[135]

Our spiritual life is one long exercise in cultivation, providing the kind of environment that is conducive to spiritual growth, and avoiding hindrances which might stunt that growth. Just as we add water, sunlight, and fertilizer, and remove weeds and rocks, if we are serious about helping a seed to grow, there are qualities we need to give attention to. Notice Peter's promise:

> For if these things are in you, and abound, they will make you neither barren nor unfruitful in the knowledge of our Lord Jesus Christ.[136]

To be a disciple of Christ is to be a perpetual learner, one who remains under instruction, a trainee—an apprentice. We put our Learner Plates on when we first believe, and we keep them on for the rest of our lives.

We are familiar with Jesus' last instructions to his followers: make disciples and baptise them in the name of the Father, the Son, and the Holy Spirit.[137] But the next verse contains an additional directive: "and teach them to observe all that I commanded you." The word "teach" also implies "train", "coach" or "mentor". When Jesus asked to "teach them all I have commanded you", he referred to both his words and his works. Christian discipleship is both proclamation and demonstration.

Paul explains the reason for proclaiming Christ and teaching believers: "That we may present every man complete [mature] in Christ".[138] Simply to lead someone to salvation without teaching him God's Word and ways is equivalent to leaving a new-born

---

135   Monty Don, *Down to Earth*, 152-3
136   2 Peter 1:5-8
137   Matthew 28:19-20
138   Colossians 1:28

baby to fend for itself. Salvation is only the start of a believer's walk with the Lord. It is the first step in a lifelong process of learning in order to grow to spiritual maturity.

We should not limit the task of teaching to church leaders and evangelists any more than we should say that they alone are responsible for evangelising the lost. The entire body of Christian believers is given the assignment of making disciples and teaching them the ways of the Lord. Instead of just sitting in church meetings, waiting to be fed more truth for our own benefit, the Lord expects us to disciple others by passing on to them what we have been taught and trained to do.

When we consider how much we have been taught after we were saved, what can we share with others that will help them to put down deeper roots and grow in Christ?

Our heavenly Father is concerned for the nurture and development of his children. He wants his children to receive the benefits of a good education. Therefore, he has enrolled every one of his children in a school of his choice, the lifelong school of the Spirit. Disinterested learners make poor disciples, but "a wise son makes his father's heart glad."[139]

> Instruct a wise man and he will be wiser still; teach a righteous man and he will add to his learning.[140]

> He who learns from instruction and correction is on the [right] path of life [and for others his example is a path toward wisdom and blessing], but he who ignores and refuses correction goes off course [and for others his example is a path toward sin and ruin].[141]

Natural ability alone will take us only so far, but with training we can be taken to a higher level of excellence. It takes training and skill to work smarter.

Remember: the duller the axe the harder the work. Use your head: the more brains, the less muscle.[142]

---

139   Proverbs 10:1
140   Proverbs 9:9
141   Proverbs 10:17 Amplified Version
142   Ecclesiastes 10:10 The Message version

God's Training Programme

It has been said that the Christian life can be described as consisting of three Cs: the call, the college, and the commission. We are called by the Lord to be followers of Christ, and we are given a specific purpose to pursue as witnesses to Christ. We are commissioned, authorised and released to activate that call. But between the call and the commission is the college: the training process to equip us for ministry and service. The quality of our witness is dependent upon our commitment to the process of preparation appointed by the Holy Spirit.

The word "preparation" in New Testament Greek is *katartismos*,[143] which means "preparation", "equipping", "to make ready", "to furnish completely", "make fit for use", "set in order", "set a broken bone", "mend nets to make ready for fishing", "to prepare for war", "perfecting" and "completing". It is associated with making a believer fully qualified through training, mentoring, coaching, and impartation. In other words, preparation is an essential feature of making, maturing and mobilising disciples of Jesus Christ. God wants us to do his work, done in his way, in his timing, which will produce his results.

In Isaiah 49 there is a good allusion to the twofold preparation required for formation into Christlikeness: character and ministry.

> The Lord called me from the womb, from the body of my mother he named my name. He made my mouth like a sharp sword; in the shadow of his hand he hid me; he made me a polished arrow; in his quiver he hid me away. And he said to me, "You are my servant, Israel, in whom I will be glorified."[144]

The prophet pictures an arrow and he says that the shaft of the arrow must be polished before its use. The shaft is one of the arrow's important components. If it is warped or misaligned, it will miss its mark. A crooked shaft makes the arrow useless. On the other hand, the arrow would be useless if it reached its target but the arrowhead was too blunt to penetrate the target. The

---

143   *Strong's Concordance*, 2677
144   Isaiah 49:1-3

shaft and head are equally important. While the shaft speaks of our character, the head speaks of our ministries. Both the character and the ministry of God's servant need to be properly prepared. Isaiah said that God had made him to be a polished shaft. The wooden shaft needs to undergo a process of being cut and separated from the parent wood, stripped of its bark, straightened, sanded and polished before it could play its role. Acacia wood was often used in biblical times because of its strength and durability, but it was notorious for being rough, crooked and knotted. It had to be carefully straightened and sanded. After first being stripped of its leaves and bark, the naked piece of wood was subjected to a long process of being left in a frame using tightly placed pegs that would slowly straighten the wood. Eventually, after a period of waiting and constant pressure, the straightened shaft would be oiled—anointed—to soften the wood before the final sanding. After sanding, which made the shaft smoothed and polished, it was ready to be fitted with its sharp head.

He made me a polished arrow.

Every serious disciple of Jesus Christ will experience character preparation, the straightening of the shaft, and ministry preparation, the sharpening of the head. Our ministries are only as good as our character. The Lord takes his disciples through stripping, straightening and polishing, which can be a painful and long process. The more God plans to use an arrow the more demanding will be its preparation.

Isaiah 49 gives one final stage in the preparation process: "In his quiver he hid me away". We might think that after the preparation of the head and shaft were complete the arrow would be used immediately. Not so. After shaping the character and honing the ministry skills there is a test: the patience test. Visibility gives credibility. Ask any public figure. Yet the Lord may hide us away from visibility and require us to wait until his timing for activation. This tests the believer's heart. Does he or she truly desire to serve the Lord for God's glory or for his or her own glory?

We need to understand that God has a perfect timing, when,

like an arrow, he releases us to hit the targets he has ordained for us. Jesus was sent forth in the fullness of time. God has a special season of hiding us in his quiver and another one for releasing us at his appointed time. Temptations and pressure will come to all of us to move ahead of God's timing. There is no set pattern for every disciple to follow. The timing and method of God's release are different for everyone. Every believer is different and God gives different callings and different levels of influence. None of us should compare ourselves with others. Peter was wrong to compare himself to John. We need to learn how to wait patiently for the Lord's timing.

> By faith and patience we inherit the promises of God.[145]

Even for the great men and women of the Bible, preparation never ended. There are no shortcuts. Maturity is not attained in a moment. They were never complete in their preparation but they were always growing into their callings.

Promotion through Submission

> *Eternal God,*
> *the light of the minds that know you,*
> *the joy of the hearts that love you,*
> *and the strength of the wills that serve you;*
> *grant us to know you*
> *that we may truly love you,*
> *so to love you that we may truly serve you,*
> *whose service is perfect freedom;*
> *through Jesus Christ our Lord. Amen.*[146]

Elisha was called of God to succeed the great revivalist prophet, Elijah. Before he was commissioned and released into his ministry, he was required to serve his mentor as his personal body-servant. Jesus, though he was God in the flesh, was required to obey his earthly parents, attend a synagogue school and the temple,

---

145   Hebrews 6:12
146   After St Augustine of Hippo

learn a trade, hold down a job to earn an income, and, when his stepfather Joseph died, provide for his mother, brothers and sisters as head of the family. Father God required that his divine Son submit to a lengthy process of character formation during these hidden years. Only when thirty years of the preparation process were complete did the Father release Jesus into public ministry. By then Jesus was totally convinced that he was not meant to pursue his ministry but to serve the ministry of his Father. He was utterly surrendered to the principle of submission —under the mission of his Father.[147] It is the same with us. In the apprenticeship season, the Lord promotes his disciples by testing their hearts as to whether they are willing to serve or not.

> If then you have not been faithful with the unrighteous wealth, who will entrust to you the true riches? And if you have not been faithful with that which is another's, who will give you that which is your own?[148]

Another Bible version renders this verse as:

> So if you have not been trustworthy in handling worldly wealth, who will trust you with true riches? And if you have not been trustworthy with someone else's property, who will give you property of your own?[149]

These verses allude to two credibility tests. They are two ways God seeks to form fruitful and productive disciples. Firstly, if we cannot steward our finances and material provisions well, why should God entrust us with greater riches, spiritual gifts, and anointings? And secondly, if we are to be entrusted with a ministry of our own, we first need to prove our integrity by coming under and serving another's godly ministry.

We see this principle of promotion operating throughout the Bible with such people as Joseph, Joshua, Samuel, David, Elisha,

---

147   John 5:19-20, 30
148   Luke 16:12 ESV
149   NIV

the twelve apostles and the seventy disciples, Paul, Timothy, Titus, Silas, and of course, Jesus himself.

The Proving Ground

The "college" of the Holy Spirit is God's proving ground. An inspirational example in the Bible is Joseph. He received his call from God at the age of seventeen through two dreams, but he did not graduate into the commission of his call until he was thirty. Between the call and the commission were thirteen years in the college of the Holy Spirit. The major elements of God's training programme were tests and trials. He was subjected to betrayal, abandonment, slavery, false accusation and imprisonment. His curriculum was pressure and proving. Psalm 105 says,

> He sent a man before them, Joseph, who was sold as a slave. His feet they hurt with shackles; He was put in chains of iron, until the time that his word [of prophecy regarding his brothers] came true, the word of the Lord tested and *refined* him[150] . . . the word of the Lord proved him true.[151]

The Old Testament Hebrew word used here is *tsaraph*,[152] which means to "refine", "purge", "try", "smelt", "fit for service", or "test and prove by means of suffering". Gideon's men were tested, and as a result only three hundred were chosen. There are times when the personal word God gives us will act as a proving ground, putting us to the test, trying and stretching us to become strong and mature enough to carry the word through obedience.

It is a leadership principle that credibility comes from visibility. To be denied visibility before the people will negatively affect a leader's value and credibility.

During Joseph's years of slavery and imprisonment, God severely limited his visibility. It was in these hidden years that the shaft of Joseph's character was straightened and the arrowhead of his anointing was sharpened. Joseph became a fit tool in the

---

150   Psalm 105:17-19 Amplified Version
151   NIV
152   *Strong's Concordance*, 6884

hand of God, and, at the right time, God promoted him from the prison to the palace. It is worth noting that when Joseph tried to take matters into his own hands and accelerate God's timing by urging the cupbearer and baker to speak to Pharaoh for him, the waiting time was extended by a further two years. Joseph had tried to move ahead of God. The way to success was attained by the path of pressure. Joseph's call from God, at age seventeen, had to fit him. He had to grow into the calling, just as a child has to grow to fit adult-sized clothes. The word "proved" can also mean "fitted". Verse 19 can be rendered *"till the word of the Lord fitted him."* The call had to fit Joseph. It is God's mercy not to release us into any weighty responsibility until we have the character to fit it. We would not agree to infant weddings or infant senior management posts. With responsibility comes accountability. To save us from being under judgment, God will not release us before time into such responsibilities. Man proposes but God disposes. The best thing God can do is to withhold success until we are ready. Promotion in the kingdom of God comes when we are able to handle God's dealings correctly, proving our attitudes under great testing.

> For you, God, tested us; you refined us like silver. You brought us into prison and laid burdens on our backs. You let people ride over our heads; we went through fire and water, but you brought us to a place of abundance.[153]

God is a refiner, a prover, and he tests his saints.

> The crucible for silver and the furnace for gold, but the Lord tests the heart.[154]

His promotions, the abundance, come when character is developed and proven stable in the crucible of his fiery trials. The Lord fires up his friends!

---

153 Psalm 66:10-12 NIV
154 Proverbs 17:3

The Crucible

Precious metals are refined through a process of intense heat and pressure. The Bride of Christ is destined to appear before her Bridegroom God without spot or wrinkle. Even prostitutes can become brides. Dirt spots and smudges on a garment are removed only by a laundry process of rubbing and scrubbing. The wrinkles are then removed by ironing, which requires intense heat and pressure. This is a major function of the Holy Spirit to prepare the Bride of Christ for the return of her Lord. Cleansing, heat, and pressure are activities employed by the Holy Spirit with God's friends.

Pressure is able to produce godliness. It reveals strength of character and presents us with opportunities for growth. Adversity is a tool in the hand of God. He uses it to strengthen real faith by causing believers to dig down deep into God. People think that believing in God will make them immune from adversity, but Jesus told us that we shall have trouble and we are required to carry a cross as his disciples. Not all hardships are the result of our sins or spiritual attacks; they can be also a consequence of carrying our cross and following Christ. Friendship with God means cross-carrying. When such trials come from the will of God, then it is totally inappropriate to bind and loose or take authority over the situation. We cannot take authority over Christ or bind the cross. We would be fighting from the wrong corner. Our proper response is to acknowledge and embrace the trial as an instrument of God. This was the lesson God's friend, Job, was required to learn, and so too are we. It has been said that there are only two proper responses to God: enjoy or endure. We are either in a season of enjoying, and if not, then we are in a season of enduring.

Tests and Trials

Although the apostle Paul experienced times of exultation and delight with the Lord, there were many times when he would have had to endure hardships and suffering. He described three types of trial to be endured: troubles, hardships, and distresses.[155] The New Testament Greek words for these three trials are: *thlipsis*,[156] which means "trouble", "affliction", "burdened", "persecution" or "tribulation", *anagkais*,[157] which means "hardship", "constraint", "painful necessity", "requirement" or "under pressure", *stenochoriais*,[158] which means "distress", "anguish", "calamity", "in a tight spot" or "confined". Suffering is always part of the offering in a believer's life. "Take up your cross . . . and follow me."[159]

Pressure squeezes the true condition of our hearts on the surface. Gethsemane means an "oil press", a place for squeezing the oil from olives. An olive press is a device that puts olives under great pressure in order to release the oil within. Jesus was put under great pressure in Gethsemane, and the pressure manifested the anointing that was upon his life as Saviour of the world. Pressure, adversity, trials and tests are some of the ways God employs to form us into the likeness of Christ.

> We must go through many hardships to enter the kingdom of God.[160]

Someone once said, "If you don't have problems, perhaps you should get on your knees and ask, 'Lord, don't you trust me?'" Wisdom teaches us that not all pain and trouble are wholly evil in purpose, but ladders to be climbed onto spiritual maturity.

The Test of Time

Pain is unavoidable in this life. There will always be times of heartache and tragedy. Betrayal, desertion and unfaithfulness are common experiences both to man and God. But it is what we do with these experiences that determines the kind of people we allow ourselves to become. We are the people we choose to be.

---

155   2 Corinthians 6:4-5
156   *Strong's Concordance*, 2347
157   *Strong's Concordance*, 318
158   *Strong's Concordance*, 4730
159   Matthew 16:24
160   Acts 14:22

The Bible says, "As a man thinks within himself, so he is."[161] Every challenge sets before us a choice to become either bitter or better. In God's economy, these occasions are intended to serve as grace growers in our lives. Esau had plotted brother's death. Instead, we see Esau embracing Jacob when they meet many years later. That must have been difficult for Esau. But time away from each other had helped heal the bitter wounds and enable the two brothers to see how their relationship with each other was more important than the hurts of their past rivalries. Time can be a healer.

God's Timing

> Be still before the Lord and wait for him.[162]

Timing is everything in comedy. God is perfect in all his ways, so his timing is immaculate: he is always on time, never too early or too late. God's success is in his timing. He has a set time for his plans: "At the set time of which God had spoken."[163] God's will, done in God's time, brings success. His ways are not our ways, and his timing is not always what we would want to choose for ourselves. He operates in *chronos*[164] time, the linear measurement of time in minutes and hours, but his actions are dictated by *kairos*[165] time—time spent purposefully, intentionally, an opportune time, in due season.[166] There is a right and a wrong time to act. God thinks in seasons. To move in the will of God requires moving in the right time. Jesus berated his blood brothers because they operated in their own time and not in God's timing. Jesus said, "The right time for me has not yet come; for you any time is right."[167]

---

161 Proverbs 23:7 NIV
162 Psalm 37:7 NRSV
163 Genesis 21:2
164 *Strong's Concordance*, 5550
165 *Strong's Concordance*, 2540
166 Ephesians 5:16
167 John 7:6 NIV

We are used to thinking about managing time and being on time. Waiting for a train, getting the children to school, arriving for an interview, schedules, timelines and timetables are understood as necessary for the successful outcome of enterprises. In all fields of life, there are some situations which demand specific and non-negotiable timings even as a matter of life and death. The cry of the Christian message is "Now is the acceptable [*kairos*] hour".[168] There is sense of maturing and ripeness of time when it comes to the affairs of God's kingdom. In one of his parables, Jesus used an agricultural analogy to reveal that there is a right and wrong time to act.[169] There is also a right time to make preparations before taking action. There is a time to sit at Jesus' feet, as Mary and Martha learned, but there is also a right time when the Lord says, "Don't hold on to me . . . Instead, go."[170]

It is all too easy to impose our preconceived timetable upon God's promises, but we will find it difficult to deal with the frustration and anxiety that result when God does not answer "on time" according to our expectations. Jesus frequently referred to his own mission in terms of "This is not my hour . . . This is my hour." The practice of recognising God's timing and being patient in waiting upon him is essential if we are to stay in step with his plans and purposes. There will be many occasions when the Lord will require us to pass the test of time. Delays, far from being a failing, can be deliberately orchestrated by God. The Lord tarries. These can be times of frustration and disappointment for us, if we are insensitive to his purposes. We may find it easier to appreciate that the return of Christ tarries for the sake of the realisation of the full number of the elect. Yet we can be really challenged when meeting our own immediate needs tarries. We have to understand that our lives impinge on others and that meeting the needs of others often coincides with the timing of meeting our needs.

---

168   2 Corinthians 6:2
169   Matthew 13:24-30
170   Luke 10:41-42, John 20:17

Reasons for Delay

There are times when the Lord will delay for the sake of achieving greater works. The limitation of our vision can produce false expectations of outcome and timing but God is working at a different agenda from what we expect. God's delays can then seem frustrating and disappointing, because our vision is too limited. Christ's response to Jairus' plea to rescue his daughter from death was majorly delayed by a woman with a haemorrhage.[171] In the event, the Lord's purpose was not healing but a greater work, raising the dead. The same was true of Jesus' treatment of Lazarus.[172] Instead of responding earlier, when he was called by the family to heal their brother, Jesus delayed in order to do a greater work. The *I Am* was revealed in greater glory as *The Resurrection*.

The Lord can often delay his responses to us not because we are in error or needing to be corrected but because he has a bigger purpose to fulfil in our lives. There are occasions when the Lord appears to move slowly, if at all. But even if his promises may not come speedily, they will certainly come!

Accelerate or Brake?

We may pray or prophesy, expecting the Lord to release accelerated growth, speeding up the process of our personal development and spiritual maturation. We are desirous for the hastening of time. But we may need to exercise caution when our zeal runs ahead believing that God wants to us to be blessed with a time of acceleration. Sometimes this desire comes more from the flesh than the spirit, as we are looking for quick-fix solutions. God can and does provide accelerated growth but not in response to our impatience or indolence. There is a danger in haste just as there is in tardiness. Jesus highlighted these dangers in the parable of the wise and foolish bridesmaids and the parable of the talents.

---

171 Mark 5:21-43
172 John 11

There are times when the right response is to take things slowly and not to quicken the pace. We need to take our time to assimilate and consolidate fully what God wants to do in us. There are times when acceleration would be a big mistake. Instead, we will need to hold our ground and dig deep into the fruits of the Holy Spirit. We must remember that though gifts are given in a moment, fruits are grown and take time to mature. The things of the Spirit require patience, not haste. Good and lasting things take time to grow. Therefore, the will of God may not be to apply the accelerator but the brake.

Withholding Love

There are times when the Lord may choose to withhold things from his friends. We rejoice in the truth that the Lord is our Friend and Provider (*Jehovah-jireh*), but have we reckoned that part of providing for us is to withhold from us? There are times when the full flood of his provision could have a devastating effect, like a torrent flowing from a broken dam.

As consumers of God's provisions, always giving to us may "spoil the child" and encourage us to be ungrateful. Undervaluing or taking God's friendship for granted could set us up for corruption and spiritual bankruptcy. Therefore, as a true friend, the Lord will be concerned for the capacity of our souls. If he did not withhold from us, we would be subject to his judgment. God withholding from us is in fact the covering hand of God's protective love, his mercy triumphing over his judgment. For example, God protects us by withholding the full revelation of himself.

As he said to his friend, Moses,

> "You cannot see my face, for no one may see me and live." Then the Lord said, "There is a place near me where you may stand on a rock. When my glory passes by, I will put you in a cleft in the rock and cover you with my hand until I have passed by."[173]

As God's friends, there is always a place for us near him and

---

173   Exodus 33:19-23 NKJV

times of delay are in fact the acts of his maintaining, preserving and protective love.

> Then the Lord came down in a cloud and stood there with him and proclaimed his name, the Lord. And he passed in front of Moses, proclaiming, "The Lord, the Lord, the compassionate and gracious God, slow to anger, abounding in love and faithfulness, maintaining love to thousands, and forgiving wickedness, rebellion and sin."[174]

Incubating Faith

Often faith needs to develop and mature before it can be effective. There were times when Jesus had to speak to his disciples about their little faith. He was referring not so much to the size or quantity of their faith but to it being under-developed, not fully grown. There are times when God requires faith to be developed to full strength before the resources of heaven will be released on earth. The gift of faith is an impartation by the Holy Spirit of God's complete confidence in his own ability to perform a miracle. Jesus said, "Have the faith of God."[175] But the faith of God will need to be incubated in us.

On the other hand, the emphasis is not on faith being incubated to full strength, but faith needs to incubate a promise of God. It is not about what needs to be done to faith but what faith does to a situation. Although God promised Elijah rain would come after a three-year drought, Elijah still had to exercise faith and pray for the fulfilment of the promise. He prayed not once but seven times before he saw the reward of his prayers. Why the delay? The Bible describes Elijah's attitude of prayer as squatting down like a chicken incubating an egg. It took time for Elijah's prayer of faith to hatch God's promise. We are not told specifically why God delayed answering Elijah's prayer, even after God had promised him to bring the rain, but surely there are some dynamics of prayer we are intended to learn from this example. We can learn how faithful servants of God need to conduct themselves when waiting upon the Lord to act.

---

174   Exodus 34:5-7
175   Mark 11:22

One key to success in Christian life is simply giving God time to work. Rough edges take time to smooth. Growth to maturity never occurs overnight. But each day can be a step in the right direction. Like sandpaper, we need to learn to cooperate with, not oppose, the work of the Master Carpenter.

Every work of God in our lives is designed to increase our dependence on him and maintain his friendship with us. Every assignment he gives us will require his participation and pre-appointed timing in order to succeed.[176] As Paul writes, "Not that we are sufficient of ourselves to think of anything as being from ourselves, but our sufficiency is from God."[177]

---

[176] Acts 17:26-27 NKJV
[177] 2 Corinthians 3:5 NKJV

Prayer

*Lord Jesus, never let me think that I have enough knowledge
to need no teaching.
Never let me think that I have enough wisdom
to need no correction.
Never let me think that I have gifts and experience enough
that I need no grace.
Never let me think that I have enough goodness
that I need no progress.
Never let me think that I have enough humility
that I need no repentance.
Never let me think that I have enough devotion
that I do not need enlivening.
Never let me think that I have sufficient strength
without your Spirit;
for, in standing still, I fall backwards.
Never let me become self-satisfied;
never let me go, never let me off,
but continue spurring me onwards,
with your life-giving, love-filling, transforming, sanctifying
work.
Keep me enrolled in the school of your Spirit.*

6

Wrestled by God

Human beings have always wrestled with questions about the essentials of life. Why are we here? Where do we come from? Where are we going? Is there any purpose and significance to our lives beyond this life? How perplexing, then, when someone who knows God as their friend and travel companion is suddenly attacked by him. The adventure, while retaining an element of excitement, may very well seem less attractive and compelling for a season. A whole list of other questions will surface, chiefly, "I thought he was my friend. Why has he suddenly turned against me?"

> So Jacob was left alone, and a man wrestled with him till daybreak. When the man saw that he could not overpower him, he touched the socket of Jacob's hip so that his hip was wrenched as he wrestled with the man. Then the man said, "Let me go, for it is daybreak." But Jacob replied, "I will not let you go unless you bless me." The man asked him, "What is your name?" "Jacob," he answered. Then the man said, "Your name will no longer be Jacob, but Israel, because you have struggled with God and with humans and have overcome." Jacob said, "Please tell me your name." But he replied, "Why do you ask my name?" Then he blessed him there. So Jacob called the place Peniel, saying, "It is because I saw God face to face, and yet my life was spared." The sun rose above him as he passed Peniel, and he was limping because of his hip.[178]

---

[178] Genesis 32:24-31

Why Did God Choose to Wrestle with Jacob?

Jacob's wrestling match with God is one of the most intriguing stories in the Bible. The story is often referred to as Jacob wrestling with God, but it would be more accurate to say that God wrestled with Jacob. God took the initiative in coming as an anonymous man to wrestle with Jacob. There is no doubt in Jacob's mind that this was an encounter with God himself. He named the place "Peniel", which means "face of God", saying "It is because I have seen God face to face and yet my life was spared."[179]

As to why God chose to wrestle with Jacob, we are not told directly, but the details of the story hint at the answer. Perhaps Jacob needed to wrestle with God instead of himself or others. The struggle lasted all night. Jacob held his own, but the mysterious wrestler wasn't willing to shorten the conflict and the hardship to Jacob. The struggle came to an end when with just a touch the Lord dislocated Jacob's hip, wounding and causing great pain, and demonstrating that he could have easily defeated Jacob at any time. This was a lesson in humility—showing Jacob his need of God. As a permanent reminder of the meeting, Jacob would live the rest of his life with a limp. Every step he would take would remind him of his struggle with God. Though Jacob suffered through this encounter, he did something truly brave and remarkable. He refused to give up until God gave him a blessing. He continued to fight, but now it was for God, not against God.

Perhaps the reason for the encounter was to ensure that Jacob, who became Israel, had the correct motivation and attitude toward God. It was a lesson in humility, and Jacob responded by a show of faith and longing for God.

God reveals himself to us for various reasons. Among them are: to bring him glory, to increase our knowledge of him, to understand our relationship with him, and to be shaped and transformed by him. Jacob's experience accomplished all these.

---

[179] Genesis 32:30 NIV

It is an experience that is formative for all God's people, for all time.

Up to this point, Jacob had spent his entire life striving to be the captain of his own destiny, deceiving and manipulating others around him. His name means "grasper", "deceiver", "trickster". He was ruthless in his attempts to exploit others for his own advantage, causing them great pain. He deceived his father, defrauded his brother and cheated his uncle.

His life was one of never-ending struggles. Though God promised that Jacob would become not only a great nation but also a whole company of nations, Jacob was still full of fears and anxieties.

Peniel became a pivotal point in his life. He was about to meet his brother, Esau, who had vowed to kill him. All Jacob's struggles and fears were about to be realised. Disheartened by his father-in-law's treatment, Jacob had fled Laban, only to encounter his embittered brother, Esau. Afraid for his life, Jacob planned a bribe, sending a convoy of gifts along with his women and children in the hope of pacifying his brother. With his father-in-law behind him and Esau before him, he faced the dilemma of running away or facing the full fury of the brother he had cheated. Physically and emotionally spent, with the prospect of facing death, he let go of all his worldly possessions and family ties, and sought solitude in the wilderness.

Only then did his real struggle begin. That night a stranger attacked Jacob, wrestling with him all through the night until dawn. To put an end to the struggle, the stranger crippled Jacob with a disabling blow to his hip, which would cause him to walk with a limp for the rest of his life.

At the conclusion of the struggle, God blessed him and gave him a new identity, Israel, which means "one who contends with God", "a friend of God."[180]

Western culture celebrates wealth, power, strength and prestige. We disdain weakness, failure, and doubt. Though we know that a degree of vulnerability and insecurity come with

---

180   Genesis 32:29

life, we tend to view these as signs of failure or even a lack of faith. Yet we also know that in real life, all that glistens is not gold, and that temporal success can be recipe for discontent and despair. Sooner or later, the cold, hard realism of life catches up with most of us. The story of Jacob pulls us back to reality. Jacob's encounter with God at Peniel is the "magnificent defeat of the human soul at the hands of God."[181]

In Jacob's story we can recognize our own struggles, fears, darkness, emptiness, and feelings of powerlessness. The apostle Paul experienced similar discouragement and fears: "We were harassed at every turn—conflicts on the outside, fears within."[182] Yet God, who turns all things to our good, does not want to leave us with our trials. He offers us not only a way through but also gifts of freedom, endurance, faith and courage.

In the end, Jacob does what we all must do. He confronted his failures, weaknesses and sins, all the things that had been imprisoning and confining him. It was only after he came to grips with God and ceased his struggling, realising that he could not go on without God, that he received the blessing of God's friendship and leadership over his life.[183]

Jacob's life teaches that our lives are never fulfilling when we take it upon ourselves to wrestle with God and his will for our lives. As God's people, despite our trials and tribulations, our strivings are never devoid of God's presence, and his blessing inevitably follows the struggle. Real growth always involves struggle and pain.

Jacob's wrestling with God at Peniel during that dark night reminds us of this truth: though we may fight God and his will for us, in truth, God is good. We may well struggle with him through the loneliness of the night, but his blessing will come by daybreak.

Jacob had an issue with running away from his mistakes instead of confronting them head on. This ultimately took a toll on his life. God decided it was time for Jacob to confront his

---

181	Frederick Buechner, *The Magnificent Defeat*
182	2 Corinthians 7:5
183	Genesis 32:29

fears. God told him to return to the brother who had vowed to kill him. Alone and unburdened of all his possessions and family ties, he was on the horns of a dilemma: should he run away or stay to meet his brother and face the consequences? But then God appears to him as an adversary and dislocates his hip. It is too late to flee with a dislocated hip. He has no choice but to meet with his brother and confront his past failings.

Jacob had become too reliant upon his material prosperity. His motto could have been: "God helps those who help themselves." But God was showing him that this was not the way to fulfil his life's destiny. He needed to shift his focus onto God himself.

> Trust in God with all your heart and lean not on your own understanding.[184]

Doing things God's way, in God's strength, will not lack God's resources and will produce God's results. A self-made man will always depend upon his own resources, and his experience will be limited to what only his own strength can achieve. But friendship with God means we have to allow him to wrestle with us. God wrestles with his friends.

God Is Not Safe

After twenty years, God had finally caught up with Jacob. He had spent his life seeking to be blessed but avoiding God. At Peniel he was forced to meet with God, and the confrontation would change him for ever. Throughout Israel's history, as told in the Old Testament, the Jews were repeatedly forced through conflict to step forward and commit themselves afresh to God. The New Testament tells that trials develop perseverance and refine faith.[185] Today, our sentimental age rejects an aspect of God's nature: he is dangerous.[186] In this story he is the aggressor,

---

184   Proverbs 3:5-6
185   James 1:2-4, 1 Peter 1:6-7
186   Exodus 4:24. Compare this with Isaiah 6:5, Judges 13:22, Matthew 17:6, Revelation 1:17.

The Most Compelling Adventure

the antagonist. God is not always comfortable to be around! God is not tame. He cannot be controlled. He is not dangling on the end of our string. He is dangerous, and we need to respect him. T.S. Eliot called him "Christ the Tiger". Like Aslan in *The Chronicles of Narnia*, he is terrible and he is lovely, wild but loving.

> "Aslan is a lion—the Lion, the great Lion." "Ooh" said Susan. "I'd thought he was a man. Is he—quite safe? I shall feel rather nervous about meeting a lion" . . . "Safe?" said Mr Beaver . . . "Who said anything about safe? 'Course he isn't safe. But he's good. He's the King, I tell you."[187]

He is the Lamb of God, but he is also the Lion of Judah. This is part of the understanding that "the fear of the Lord is the beginning of wisdom."[188] Calvin described God "as an antagonist" who "descends into the arena to try our strength . . . God uses adversity as either a rod with which he corrects our sins, or the test of our faith and patience."[189]

Jacob the grabber was finally grabbed by God. It was exactly at a low time in Jacob's life, when he was frantic with fear of what his brother might do to him, that God attacked him, grabbing him and wrestling him to the ground. Finally, God struck "below the belt", leaving Jacob "out of joint" and in pain. But Jacob would not surrender. He struggled on, refusing to let go. With his remaining strength, he clung to his opponent for support and blessing.

This was not a matter of repentance for past sins. Jacob's fear of his brother Esau drove him to pray for God's help. Alone and helpless he sought solitude, appealing to God for help. "Save me", he pleaded.[190] But just at the time when Jacob was struggling, lonely, and in need of a friend, God decided to pick a fight with him. This sounds rather like kicking a man when he is down! God was more dangerous than Esau. As an aggressor,

---

187	C.S. Lewis, *The Lion, the Witch and the Wardrobe*, 10
188	Proverbs 9:10
189	Calvin, Genesis, Vol 2, 195-6
190	Genesis 32:11

God is more to be feared than people. As Jesus said, God is the One who is really to be feared.[191]

Why Did God Contend with Jacob?

At heart, it was a battle of wills for control. God did not answer Jacob's prayer by offering him sympathy and comfort. He came to fight him. God was not looking for a self-sufficient superman; he wanted a follower who walked with a limp. God wants limping Jacobs.

Resisting God is exhausting. All the energy spent on maintaining self-reliance is exhausting and only paves the way to spiritual bankruptcy.

We are all damaged goods in need of transformation. There are mischievous "imps" tapping at the windows of our souls, chattering "ghosts" from the past clamouring for our attention. There are unopened cupboards in the attics and basements of our souls, shadows in our hearts, where we wrestle with fears, insecurities, self-doubt, past traumas, betrayals and rejections, places where Christ's liberating light still needs to penetrate. Some people are entirely maimed because they have seen the naked face of evil and cannot look past it to any vision of goodness. Belief in an all-loving and good God is hard to sustain behind a protective skin.

Facing up to the reality of our true condition can be painful.

> Flee, flee, bird of paradise, for human kind cannot stand very much reality.[192]

People want the blessings of God, but they resent any suggestion of him interfering with their preferred lifestyles. Authenticity before God is not easy. There is a Jacob-Israel within all of us.

But acknowledging the reality of what is inside us will inevitably fail unless we are helped by the grace of God. The claim to "know thy self" is prone to self-deception, especially if

---

191   Matthew 10:28
192   TS Eliot, *Four Quartets*

such knowledge is not revealed to us through the truth of God's Word.

Jacob struggled against allowing God to hold the reins of his life. But when the wrestling had finished, his struggle against God came to an end. His change of name signified he was a changed man.

Let us return to the question: why did God see fit to wrestle Jacob? Why did God act as an aggressor toward his friend, Jacob?

As a result of the struggle Jacob became more a man of God and less his own man. After twenty years of struggling to be blessed, Jacob finally submitted himself to God. The encounter deepened his friendship and strengthened his faith in God. Yet there was more. Resistance builds strength. In combat training the trainer takes on the role of the antagonist, the aggressor. Marco Polo, the renowned Venetian adventurer to China, learned to excel in the martial arts through his coach, Hundred Eyes, who took on the role of the adversary. Though he sustained painful blows from many beatings at the beginning, he refused to give up but persisted before the onslaughts of his adversarial coach. Marco Polo learned how to resist an opponent and became a competent master.

> The Lord disciples those he loves . . . God disciplines us for our good that we may share in his holiness. No discipline seems pleasant at the time, but painful. Later on, however, it produces a harvest of righteousness and peace for those who have been trained by it.[193]

God's way is not punitive but instructive, training us for spiritual development as his beloved sons and daughters. When God wrestled with Jacob, Jacob did not lie down under the pressure. He rose to the challenge and fought back. Resistance is part of a Christian's spiritual training. "He taught my hands to war . . . We wrestle against".[194] Resistance builds strength, hardens resolve and turns us into change makers. Pressure produces

---

193   Hebrews 12:5-12
194   Psalm 144:1, Ephesians 6:12

godliness. We are not called to be thermometers, merely reflecting the status quo of the world's temperature, but thermostats, those who change the temperature.

God is God. No one is his equal. He is omnipotent, sovereign and indomitable. To say that Jacob prevailed against God can only mean that God let him win. It took just a little touch from God to cripple Jacob. The battle in Jacob's heart had been won; he had finally come to the point of acknowledging God's supremacy and worth. He clung to God for the first time and allowed him to take hold of the reins of his life. There are times when God wants his friends to wrestle him in prayer, and he lets us win. But the encounter will leave us limping, more dependent upon him. God blesses while he attacks. He is against us because he is for us. His victory is our victory.

God will sometimes challenge his beloved friends to this contest but "at the same time he will provide us with the means of resistance, so that he both fights against us and fights for us."[195] He fights against us to develop our strength and determination to be overcomers in his fight for us. It is a battle of wills, a fight for life. God will always win the wrestling match. If we are smart, the sooner we submit, the better.

It does not make sense to make an enemy of God. "It is a fearful thing to fall into the hands of the living God."[196] Even to God's friends, he can still appear to be more foe than friend. Ask Jacob about it!

"Lord, if that's the way you treat your friends, I'd hate to be your enemy!" It is no wonder God may not have many friends! God can suddenly appear to pounce on us and wrestle us to the ground, just when we are looking for some safety and security in our lives. Like Job, life is enjoyable when, suddenly, from out of sight God comes along and lobs a grenade at us. Like Jacob, our first reaction may not be entirely welcoming of the ordeal. It is not what we would naturally associate with a loving heavenly Father and Saviour. Until we receive discernment as to the source of our ordeal, we resist, fighting to get free. At some

---

195   Calvin. *Genesis, Vol 2,* 196
196   Hebrews 10:31

time during the night, Jacob realised that he was not wrestling with an enemy but with a friend. His attitude changed when he saw the ordeal as the work of his strange friend.

Once Jacob recognised the true nature of the ordeal, what was initially interpreted as a threatening experience from a foe became an incredible opportunity from a friend, and he said to God, "I will not let you go unless you bless me."[197]

---

[197] Genesis 32:26

A Prayer

Sovereign, Majestic Lord,
bring me to the end of myself and turn me fully to you.
Wrestle with me and have your way because your way is always best.
Contend with any false view of you as simply friendly, almost a benign figure
whom I can manipulate or turn to my advantage when things get difficult.
Without a healthy fear of you,
I can wrongly assume you are more for me than for yourself.
Like Jacob, I can seek to use you for my own gain in life and my own wants.
Enter God into the mess of my life and refocus my mind that you are not a God to be manipulated
but a God to be worshiped.
Turn me to the place where submission is strength—
submission to your leading and your control,
knowing that there is nothing stronger.
Make me a man dependent upon God,
rather than dependent upon himself.
Renew me by your power,
remade in your image,
fully surrendered to your will for my life.

7

The Way of Silence and Stillness

The Lord your God is in your midst . . . he will quiet you by his love.[198]

Find rest, O my soul, in God alone.[199]

Wait for the Lord, and keep his way. He will exalt you to inherit.[200]

Almighty God,
You have made us for yourself,
And our hearts are restless until they find their rest in you:
Pour your love into our hearts and draw us to yourself,
And so bring us at last to your heavenly city
Where we shall see you face to face;
Through Jesus Christ our Lord. Amen.

The Mysteries of God's Silences

Between good friends silence can be as eloquent and enjoyable as verbal sharing. Silence is golden, as they say, but not to those who are afraid of being alone. Those who find it difficult to cope with themselves can feel threatened by silences and welcome the distraction of noise and clamour. They seek to avoid the journey inwards because it can lead to a recognition of their

---

[198] Zephaniah 3:17
[199] Psalm 62:5
[200] Psalm 37:34

inner emptiness and loneliness. Fear of encountering their inner loneliness drives them to fill their lives with noise and voices. In our industrialised age, we are rightly concerned about air pollution but what about noise pollution?

T.S. Eliot analysis of modern culture led him to write,

> Where shall the word be found, where will the word resound? Not here, there is not enough silence . . . The right time and the right place are not here. No place of grace for those who avoid the face. No time to rejoice for those who walk among noise and deny the voice.[201]

People have difficulty with silence, because it makes them feel helpless, out of control. They rely on words in an attempt to manage and control their circumstances and other people. But in silence we are freed to let God be God—to let God take the reins.

> Be still, and know that I am God.[202]

Those who have been set free will embrace the discipline of inner stillness and silence and take control of the tongue.

> Real silence, real stillness, really holding one's tongue comes only as the sober consequence of spiritual stillness.[203]

Silence is one of the most significant disciplines of the Spirit.

Jesus would frequently seek "heart solitude" and communion with the Father. He commenced his ministry only after spending forty days alone in the wilderness.[204] The Scripture makes it clear that it was the initiative of the Holy Spirit driving him to a place of solitude. He spent all night alone in the hills before appointing the twelve.[205] When he heard the news of John the Baptist's death, he retreated to a solitary place.[206] After

---

201 TS Eliot, "Ash Wednesday", Stanza 5, from Collected Poems
202 Psalm 46:10
203 Dietrich Bonhoeffer, *Life Together*, 79
204 Luke 4:1
205 Luke 6:12
206 Matthew 14:13

miraculously feeding the five thousand, he withdrew to the hills by himself.[207] When the twelve apostles returned from a mission trip, he sought to take them to a place of solitude, saying to them "Come apart by yourselves."[208] After the healing of a leper, he withdrew to the wilderness for prayer.[209] Taking three of the apostles, he sought silence on a lonely mountain as a prelude to the transfiguration.[210] Preparing for the greatest challenge of his life, Jesus sought solitude in Gethsemane. And his word to all his believers is, "Come, follow me." We need to "come apart", or we will come apart!

Silence is not simply refraining from speaking; it is focusing the heart to hear and see God. The letter of James identifies the need to control the tongue, and this includes the discipline of silence. There is "a time to keep silence and a time to speak."[211] Self-control is one of the fruits of the Holy Spirit. An uncontrolled mouth is the act of a rash behaviour of a foolish believer, says Ecclesiastes.

> Guard your steps when you go to the house of God. To draw near to listen is better than to offer the sacrifice of fools, for they do not know that they are doing evil. Be not rash with your mouth, nor let your heart be hasty to utter a word before God, for God is in heaven and you are on earth. Therefore let your words be few.[212]

When Moses and Elijah appeared with Jesus and conversed with him, Peter interrupted, seeking to offer his own opinion, though no one was talking to him. He was offering the sacrifice of fools. His responsibility was to watch, listen and learn. When the cloud of God removed Jesus from his sight, the voice of God was heard to say, "Listen to him!"[213]

Silence is golden, but it is not a welcome relief when we are waiting for an answer from God, and he keeps silent. In such

---

207	Matthew 14:23
208	Mark 6:31 KJV
209	Luke 5:16
210	Luke 22:39-46
211	Ecclesiastes 3:7
212	Ecclesiastes 5:1-2
213	Matthew 17:5

times, our prayer might well be as the psalm says, "O God, do not keep silence; do not hold your peace or be still, O God!"[214] There may have been times in our lives when it felt like God was nowhere to be found, but looking back we can see that he was there and there was a reason for his silence. This can entice us to explore this mysterious silence of God.

There are numerous examples of God's people having to endure God's silence. Classic among them is Joseph. He was abused and abandoned, then sold into slavery by his brothers.[215] What he must have suffered when God was silent during the long trip to Egypt, his years as a slave, and when he was falsely accused of attempted rape and thrown into prison! Yet in all this, he experienced favour, prison led to the palace, and in the end he saved a nation and his own family.

Job, Jonah, David, Jesus in the Garden of Gethsemane. There are many examples of God's people feeling the silence of heaven. Even in Revelation, there was a whole half-hour of silence in heaven when the seventh seal was opened.[216] Yet in every situation God was present and turned every situation to their advantage.

The Silences of God

> Man shall not live by bread alone but by every word that comes from the mouth of God.[217]

> Faith comes by hearing, hearing the word of God.[218]

> The voice of the Lord is powerful; the voice of the Lord is majestic.[219]

> There is a time for everything . . . a time to be silent and a time to speak.[220]

---

214   Psalm 83:1
215   Genesis 37
216   Revelation 8:1
217   Matthew 4:4
218   Romans 10:17
219   Psalm 29:4
220   Ecclesiastes 3:1, 7

The Way of Silence and Stillness

We are used to thinking about God speaking and the importance of hearing his voice but what of his silences? Psalms frequently refer to times when God is silent. We may be familiar with reading in Scripture how God calls us to be silent.

> The Lord is in his holy temple; let all the earth be silent before him . . . Be still, and know that I am God . . . Guard your steps when you go to the house of God. Go near to listen rather than to offer the sacrifice of fools.[221]

At times, God calls for us to be silent before him and at other times he himself chooses to keep silent.

> Have I not held my peace, even for a long time? . . . Why, O Lord, do you stand far away? Why do you hide yourself in times of trouble?[222]

The temptation in these times of God's silence is to think that he has abandoned us, closed his ears to us, and no longer cares about us.

> My God, my God, why have you forsaken me? Why are you so far from saving me, from the words of my groaning? O my God, I cry by day, but you do not answer, and by night, but I find no rest.[223]

We tend to lose patience when we do not see God working in our own timeframe.

> How long, O Lord? Will you forget me for ever? How long will you hide your face from me?[224]

At moments like these, it is good to recall David's counsel, "Wait on the Lord; be of good courage, and He shall strengthen your heart; wait, I say, on the Lord!"[225]

We are used to being taught that answers to prayer are like

---

221   Habakkuk 2:20, Psalm 46:10, Ecclesiastes 5:1-2
222   Isaiah 57:11 ESV; Psalm 10:1 ESV
223   Psalm 22:1 ESV
224   Psalm 13:1 ESV
225   Psalm 83:1 NKJV

the three traffic lights: Go means *Yes*. Wait means *Not yet*. Stop means *No*. In fact we can learn so much from God's silences. His silences are intentional and can be most eloquent. We would do well to understand the Spirit's way of silence and his various reasons for it.

There are times when God's silences in the Bible were associated with negatively expressing his displeasure and judgment because the people had dishonoured him by their unwillingness to listen to him.[226] Likewise, in Amos' time, a famine of God's word or voice was seen as a disaster! God punished by his silence.[227] These occasions signified the withdrawal of his presence and his refusal to answer prayer. As a consequence, he would remove his guidance, protection and provision. In such cases his silence was seen as a calamity.[228]

Even though God uses silence to express his displeasure, nevertheless there are many other and mostly positive reasons why God uses the way of silence in the school of the Spirit. Here are some:

Reliance upon His Nature

Seasons of God's silence can be transformative in awakening us to a greater reliance upon him and beckon us to exercise our faith muscles with what we already profess to know of his nature. There are times when our heads and our hearts are not united or synchronised. We may profess to believe in God's provision and protection but it is in the test of silence that faith is proved.[229]

Reactive or responsive

We cannot hear God's voice when we are emotionally highly charged with excitement or agitation. If breakthroughs are to found in rest and quietness, then worry and fear act as growth inhibitors.[230] The noise of our emotions can act as static upon

---

226	1 Samuel 2:30, 3:1	
227	Amos 8:11-12	
228	Psalms 88:14, 143:1-2, 7, 59:39, 28:1, 35:22, 39:12, 83:1	
229	Psalm 105:17-19	
230	Isaiah 30:15	

our spiritual "TV receivers" and drown out the whispers of God in our ears. There was a time when Elisha was unable to function competently in his prophetic office because of his anger. His remedy was to call a musician to help soothe his emotions and position him rightly to hear the voice of the Lord.[231]

Go with What You Already Have

There may be times when we are overly fond of asking the Lord to do a "new thing" among us, when what we truly need is to consolidate what he has already said and revealed to us either in Scripture or by *rhema* words. The answer to what we currently need to know can be already available to us, and the Lord is silent because he wants us to value and dig deeper into what he has previously given. Are we putting that talent to good use, or have we buried it? Are we learning to steward the words he shares with us well?[232] There may be occasions when we are so attracted to seeking personal prophetic words that the authority of the written Word is being neglected.[233] The need may be to focus on what is still relevant from a past word rather than to ask for the new thing.

Dialogue Is Desired

The way of the Lord is encounter, dialogue and exchange. He frequently operates through the process of questions and answers. There are times when the Lord is waiting for us to take the initiative in asking him questions before he will speak. At other times, he will take the initiative in opening the conversation, but he waits for us to respond and extend the dialogue by asking further questions.[234] This will be treated more extensively in chapter 8. The silence of God can prompt us to ask questions. He will break his silence when we enquire and consult with him, as David discovered.

---

231   2 Kings 3:11-16
232   Jeremiah 6:16
233   Luke 16:31
234   Zechariah 4:1-5

Develop Sensitivity of Hearing

God's silence can be his way of getting us to cultivate the practice of silence, stillness and attentiveness in our lives. We engage in more active listening and develop a more accurate listening ear. The voice of heaven said, "Listen to him."[235] We cannot listen to God if we are doing all the talking. A person who enjoys the sound of his own voice is unable to appreciate others' voices, including God's. Our spiritual habit may be to bombard the Lord with lots of words, but we hardly give him room to speak.[236] The ability to recognise God's whispers becomes extremely difficult. There are times when we need to be reminded to value the Lord's voice and seek his superior wisdom.[237]

Cease Striving

The Lord's objective is to get us to learn to rest in him and stop striving in self-effort, seeking to earn approval and favour.[238] Faith is a five-letter word spelled peace. God is the God of peace, and he dwells in peace. Those who dwell in faith live in peace and enter his rest. This is about handing over control to God and allowing ourselves to be drawn into the place of peace.[239] It is from faith's place of peace and rest that the Lord wants his people to respond to, and not react against, their circumstances, living above and not under them.

Open Eyes

The silence of God could be signalling to us that we are limiting how he wishes to communicate with us. There may be an over-dependency on hearing to the neglect of seeing in the realm of the Spirit. He may be calling our attention to this deficiency and wanting us to develop our seeing capacity. The prophet Elisha prayed, "O Lord, open his eyes so he may see."[240] The

---

235 Matthew 17:5
236 Ecclesiastes 5:1-3, Matthew 6:7
237 Proverbs 1:1-7
238 Psalm 46:10
239 John 14:27, 16:33
240 2 Kings 6:17; compare with Ephesians 1:18.

problem is not having eyes but not opening them to see. Seers see!

Likewise, there may be a need to address our hearing faculty. There is a cloud of concealment, a blindfold of God, where our hearing faculty is made more acute. Blind people can develop a more acute hearing sense.

Stillness and Rest

When God speaks to us, he normally speaks in a small voice to the ears of our hearts. He is Spirit and he speaks from his Spirit to our spirit.

The Scripture describes the experience of God encountering a dejected Elijah:

> After the earthquake came a fire, but God was not in the fire. After the fire, came a still, small voice.[241]

Elijah was used to God revealing himself in mighty and dramatic ways, but God required something new from him. He wanted Elijah to hear him in the still and small.

The Old Testament Hebrew word for "still" is *dmamah*, and it carries the further meanings of "quiet", "calm", and "silent". The Hebrew word for "small" is *daq*, and it also means "crushed small or thin" or "a very little thing". The sense is to speak softly, or under the breath with a whisper, so as to be heard only by one in close proximity. God's still, small whispers require intimacy. God wants us, like Elijah, to recognise his nearness when there are no spiritual earthquake experiences to capture our attention. His love summons us to enter a more refined and intimate relationship, where he does not need to shout at us. It has been said, "The further away someone is, the more God has to shout."

God speaks softly, and we need to become still, quiet, and attentive to hear his whispers. It has also been said, "God meets man from underneath, and man must stoop to greet him."

---

[241] 1 Kings 19:12

God's command is,

> Be still, and know that I am God . . . In repentance and rest is your salvation, in quietness and trust is your strength . . . Those who wait on the Lord shall renew their strength. They shall mount up with wings of eagles; they shall run and not grow weary, and they shall walk and not faint.[242]

For God's friends, rest is the way to breakthrough victories in the spirit. David knew this and would often practise speaking to himself, commanding his soul to wait in silence, to rest and wait longingly for God.[243] Scripture reveals a number of activities associated with "being still" before the Lord: silence, quietness, waiting, watching, listening and resting. The Bible calls us to enter the rest of the Lord.[244] The rest of God is not only an objective theological concept related to salvation by grace alone. It is also a subjective mental and emotional condition we are meant to experience in our daily walk with the Lord.

God dwells in peace. He is the God of peace, and his peace passes all understanding. He is never anxious, stressed, panicked or afraid. He is never under pressure or in a hurry. He is totally self-confident in his infinite abilities and indomitable love. He is always at rest, confident in his perfection. He dwells in eternity and is not governed by the limitations of time and space. All the past, present and future are open to his superior knowledge and majestic wisdom.

He calls his friends into his peace, his rest, where confidence is the language of his Spirit. His repeated encouragement to us is, "Be still. Do not be afraid. I am with you." To enter God's rest is to cease striving from self-effort, from trying to justify our own existence, from seeking to earn acceptance and approval, from trying to merit his favour and from seeking to earn our salvation. All these things come to us from the hand of God's undeserved grace through the blood of Christ.

---

242 Psalm 46:10, Isaiah 30:15, 40:31
243 Psalm 37:7, 62:1, 5
244 Hebrews 4:2-3, 9-11

Rest and stillness are attained when we step back from our circumstances and centre ourselves on the Lord and his love for us. Rest creates a space for positive expectation to flourish unhindered. It causes us to stand before our circumstances differently—inspired, expectant and courageous, without panic or threat. Psalm 46 begins with an earthquake and a mighty tsunami, but it concludes with God's command to be still and know him.

Our exterior world is affected by our interior life. First, we have to let God be God and take control on the inside of us, and then we shall change the way we respond to our circumstances. This is how we "reign in life". The way of God is rest, stillness and waiting with attentive listening.

Resting in stillness, far from being a passive exercise, is an active practice of waiting attentively on God and the prelude to allowing him to be more active within us. On the Mount of Transfiguration, although the cloud of God hid Jesus from the disciples' sight, nevertheless, its purpose was to open their spiritual ears to greater attentiveness.[245] Listening lies at the heart of making progress in a personal relationship with God. After the Mount of Transfiguration, Jesus led the disciples back down to the valley, where more intense engagement with the world was required. Climbing God's mountains can bring us down to earth.

How Can We Become Still?

Restlessness is one of the ailments endemic in our society. It is an assault upon maintaining friendship with God. Tension, self-consciousness, scattered thoughts, unclear mind, rushing and too much busyness are enemies of communing with God and to hearing his voice. When seeking to divert the Hebrews' attention away from God, Pharaoh's ploy was to increase their workload. Satan does the same with those who would be God's friends. Too much busyness will spiritually bankrupt us. Being still is an art to be learned. We need to grow in our ability to quiet our

---

[245] Matthew 17:5

thoughts and emotions. Until they are quieted, our internal noise and spiritual static will most likely drown out his voice.

It can be helpful to follow a relaxation exercise, where we become physically and emotionally rested and calm. We can check our breathing and use it to help us relax. *Be still and know*.

When we pray, we can take a few minutes to become centred, and proceed only after we have become still. Out of our stillness, we will sense God's presence and will be able to engage with him. The more we practise becoming still, the easier it becomes and the quicker it happens.

Using the Ears and Eyes of Our Heart

We need to learn how to live in the world of the Spirit. Jesus often exhorted people to have "ears to hear and eyes to see".[246] Paul prayed that the eyes of our heart would be opened.[247] God communicates both with words to the ears and mental images to the eyes of our hearts.

If we are going to allow our hearts to be released into the freedom of the Spirit, we must learn to live in the audio-visual world of the Holy Spirit. But first, we need to believe in the value of living in that world. We have to recognise that God wants to communicate with us, and we need to be still and attentive before him. Maybe we have been somewhat dismissive about our capacity to hear and see in the realm of the Spirit, because we have given too much credence to the rational side of our mind. But if we want to acknowledge God's ways of communicating, we need to ask God's forgiveness first for not honouring and using the gift of communication he has made available to us.

Second, we need to ask God to open our spiritual ears and eyes during our quiet times, allowing God to show us things.

Third, we need to still ourselves outwardly and inwardly, so the Holy Spirit can engage with us. If you can, lie flat on the floor and stretch all the muscles in your body. Then relax each one.

---

246   Matthew 13:9-16
247   Ephesians 1:17

Focus your mind on your breathing, inhaling deeply, holding for a short while, and then exhaling. Repeat this a few times.

With each intake of breath picture in your mind the Holy Spirit filling you with his peace. As you become still, you will sense a quiet flow of impressions coming to life within you. They will have a life of their own. Go with the flow. Think that the Holy Spirit is acting like a film projector, projecting his images upon the screen of your mind.

A common practice is to choose a Gospel story and picture the scene, as if you were part of the story. Let the scene unfold in your imagination, letting God to make it come alive with his own presence.

While focusing intently on Jesus, ask the Holy Spirit what he wants to show you and then go with the flow. He will take over and direct a flow of impressions to you, revealing a significant application for your life in the present.

Prayer

For God alone my soul waits in silence[248]
Teach me the prayer of silent contemplation,
the prayer of humility, the prayer of the heart,
where deep speaks to deep,
in that stillness where we find and know you.[249]
Teach me, Lord, that silent language, which is so eloquent.
Teach my soul to rest and remain silent in your presence:
that I may adore you in the depth of my being
and ask nothing of you except the accomplishment of your
will.
Produce in my soul that deep and simple prayer, which says
nothing
and expresses everything.
To be there before you, Lord, that's all.
To shut the eyes of my body,
to shut the eyes of my soul,
and to be still and silent,
to expose myself to you, who are there, exposed to me.
To be there before you, the Eternal Presence.[250]

---

248   Psalm 62:1
249   Psalm 46:10
250   Michel Quoist, *Prayers of Life*, 113

8

Asking Good Questions

Dialogue is beneficial for establishing and maintaining healthy relationships. Asking good questions helps it. Friendship with God operates on the same basis.

> The Lord God called to the man, "Where are you?"[251]

In the Bible, there are over 500 questions God or Jesus asked people. God's questions are profoundly intriguing: "Where are you? . . . Who do you say that I am? . . . Do you want to be well? . . . What is your name?" Why so many questions? What do the questions mean? What does it mean that we have a God who comes to us with questions?

God knows everything. But he asks questions. This seems strange. When Jesus asked Peter a question, Peter's reply was, "Lord, you know everything!"[252] If God knows everything, why does he ask questions?

In education, questions are a great tool for helping students increase their understanding and connect their learning with their lives. Since the days of Socrates, asking questions to assess students' understanding has been a core component of teaching and learning. Today, verbal questioning is so prevalent in education that it's difficult to picture a classroom in which

---
251 Genesis 3:9 NIV
252 John 21:17

The Most Compelling Adventure

a teacher is not asking questions. In fact, researchers note that verbal questioning is second only to lecturing as the most common instructional practice. It has been said that teachers ask about 300-400 questions per day and as many as 120 questions per hour.

Although teachers often use verbal questioning as a tool to evaluate students' learning, it has the potential to do much more. It can "motivate students to pay attention and learn, develop students' thinking skills, stimulate students to inquire and investigate on their own, synthesize information and experiences, create a context for exploring ideas, and enhance students' cumulative knowledge base."[253]

God knows this too. God knew where Adam was hiding in the garden, yet he called him, "Where are you?"

When God asks us a question, his purpose is for us to find the answer and not for the answer to be revealed to him. God already knows the answer. He knows that questions serve other purposes than helping us learn something. When we look at the questions Jesus asked, we find they not only set the context for learning but they also drew people's attention to something more significant, promoted self-examination, prodded his audience to delve deeper and even to show an interest in others. When God asks us a question, we really need to sit up and pay attention. When the Lord says to us, "Come now, and let us reason together",[254] we are being invited to ponder along with God himself. What an unbelievable privilege!

His questions require us to look deep into our hearts before we simply react with a quick answer. When Jesus asked Peter a question, Peter was hasty in giving an answer he thought the Lord wanted to hear.[255] Christ was after more. Someone once said, "There is more learning in the question than in the answer." Jesus understood this truth.

---

253 http://www.ascd.org/publications/educational-leadership/summer08/vol65/num09/Asking-Good-Questions.aspx
254 Isaiah 1:18
255 John 21:15

Mind and Spirit

We need to learn how God speaks. He is Spirit and he speaks Spirit to spirit.[256] He does not speak to our minds but to our spirits. It takes faith to operate in the realm of the Spirit. Faith is the step of trusting what our spirits show us over our mind. Our minds handle information; our spirits receive revelation. Our mind operates by rational, logical reasoning based on the programming of our natural education. It is constantly in need of updating. It is the product of our western logical thinking, which tends to minimise our intuitive, inspirational faculties. Our spirits are the receptacles which receive supernatural revelation, the thoughts and wisdom of God. Spiritual things are spiritually discerned by our spirits.[257] The way of spiritual transformation is by the renewal of our minds, making our minds the servants of our spirits, and not vice versa.[258]

God made us to be his vice-regents on earth—interactive partners with him. The temptation has always been to function independently of him. We are made in his likeness, but we have marred his reflection within us by our self-will. Jesus is the true image of God, and thus he is the way for all who would find their way back to God. It is the way of reliance and submission to the will of God. Following the way of Christ is the way to restoration as God's vice-regents. Jesus' way of living rested upon hearing and seeing what the Father was doing, connecting with the Father situationally, consulting and relying on the Father's wisdom.

There are times when merely asking the question is not enough, but the Lord must also supply the answer so as to guide us to respond correctly. There may be times when we are somewhat slow in understanding what God is trying to tell us. Maybe we do not really want to hear the truth. Yet God in his mercy will tell us what we need to hear, so that we can fulfil our God-given destinies.

---

256   Corinthians 2:9-16
257   1 Corinthians 2:14
258   Isaiah 55:8-9, Matthew 16:23

In every question the Lord wants to help us to understand both him and ourselves. God asked Cain, "Why are you angry?"[259] It was the Lord's redemptive love seeking to reach out to help Cain examine himself to see what he could do to change.

When Elijah was scared of Jezebel's murderous threats and ran for his life, God quizzed him, "What are you doing here?"[260] God's question to Elijah implied that he had come to Sinai for his own misguided reasons and not because God had sent him. God repeated the question but Elijah's answer was the same, indicating that he had not understood the significance of what the Lord had just done through the earthquake, wind, fire and the small voice. Elijah was battling discouragement, fear and doubt. Instead of letting him sink into self-pity, the Lord's purpose was to get Elijah to review the greatness of his God and move forward again in his own destiny.

If we truly believe the Lord knows us, we must realise the questions he asks of us have a purpose. It certainly is not because he can be forgetful and needs us to remind him. He questions us, so we might think through our choices, our responsibilities and our beliefs. When we appreciate God's way of asking questions, we will be better equipped to experience his majestic wisdom in our lives.

If God Asks Questions, Should We Also?

> David inquired of the Lord, saying, "Shall I go up to one of the cities of Judah?" And the Lord said to him, "Go up." So David said, "Where shall I go up?" And He said, "To Hebron."[261]

> Gideon said to Him, "O my lord, if the Lord is with us, why then has all this happened to us? And where are all His miracles which our fathers told us about, saying, 'Did not the Lord bring us up from Egypt?'"[262]

---

259   Genesis 4:6
260   1 Kings 19:9-13
261   2 Samuel 2:1
262   Judges 6:13

Asking Good Questions

> Then the Lord showed me four craftsmen. And I said, "What are these coming to do?"[263]

> "Ask of Me, and I will give you the nations for Your inheritance."[264]

> Thus says the Lord God, "I will let the house of Israel inquire of Me to do this for them: I will increase their men like a flock."[265]

God actively encourages us to ask, enquire and seek his counsel. Apparently even the angels ask questions of their Lord.

> Then the Angel of the Lord answered and said, "O Lord of hosts, how long will You not have mercy on Jerusalem and on the cities of Judah, against which You were angry these seventy years?" And the Lord answered the angel who talked to me, with good and comforting words.[266]

God's way is to operate in a process of dialogue and questioning.

> Ask, and it will be given to you; seek and you will find; knock and it will be opened to you.[267]

We need to learn the language of God's silences if we are to become effective and productive in our walk with him. Seasoned prophetic people are familiar with God's method of questions and answers. His way is to operate by encounter, dialogue and exchange. Often, God will show us something, but not everything, in that moment. He requires us to do some digging; to dig deeper, below the surface of his *rhema* words. The kingdom of God is like a buried treasure; we need to dig to find it.[268] The Lord waits for us to return and ask him questions about what we are seeing and hearing. On the basis of our asking, he will reveal more. Other times, he takes the initiative in asking questions,

---

263   Zechariah 1:20-21 NKJV
264   Psalm 2:8 NKJV
265   Ezekiel 36:37
266   Zechariah 1:12-13
267   Matthew 7:7
268   Matthew 13:44

with the sole intent of compelling us to dig deeper into what he is revealing to us.

Thinking Metaphorically

The Bible shows us that although there are times when God speaks plainly and simply, there are many other occasions when, in his wisdom, he chooses to speak in parables, riddles, and enigmatic speech.[269] Dreams, night communications, are by nature highly symbolic. They require discernment to test their source, their interpretation, and how they should be applied to people's lives. People use similes and metaphors frequently in their everyday speech: as strong as an ox, a sea of troubles. It is quite normal, then, for God to employ these devices in communicating with us. When we learn to recognise the function or characteristic of a symbol and apply it to dreams and visions, we will understand the meaning of a dream or vision. For instance, in Scripture a lion can mean majesty and represent the Lion of Judah. On the other hand, it can mean destruction and represent Satan as a roaring lion seeking to devour.

To function in the realm of the Spirit effectively, we need to dig below the surface and unearth a deeper meaning. To accompany Jesus in his earthly ministry, people needed to be inquisitive seekers, excavators. Much of what Jesus meant lay beneath the surface of his words. He spoke symbolically, in the metaphorical language of parables. His words created pictures, which needed to be interpreted to understand their purpose. Once the meaning and purpose of his words were unearthed, a response from the listener was required. He spoke mysteries and secrets, which were lost on people who did not delve deeper into his stories.[270] He held private conversations when he would unlock the mysteries of his words. These gatherings always consisted of the true seekers, the explorers who desired to dig for the truth.

---

269 Numbers 12:6-8, Matthew 13:10-12
270 Matthew 13:11-15

The questing believer has much in common with miners, excavators, who work below the surface "extracting the precious from the worthless".[271] God's *rhema* words are like hidden treasure waiting to be excavated.[272] Psalms emphasise the practice of meditation in conjunction with Scripture.

> I meditate on your precepts and consider your ways.[273]

The word "meditation" carries the sense of digging. David Brainerd, the 18th century missionary to New England Indians, wrote to a young minister in training,

> Give yourself to prayer, to reading and meditation on divine truths: strive to penetrate to the bottom of them and never be content with a superficial knowledge.[274]

A psalm says, "Our fathers, when they were in Egypt, did not consider Your wonderful works".[275]

The Jews often failed to appreciate God because they did not strive to dig down deep and meditate on his words and actions but contented themselves with superficial knowledge.

As the saying goes, "If you can worry, you can meditate." Meditation utilises the same mental processes as worrying but in a positive way. It is the single-minded action of pursuing a thought and allowing it to dominate our perspective. The practice of digging into revelation from God raises us to a greater level of excellence.

> I have more insight than my teachers, for I meditate on your statutes.[276]

> The unfolding [opening up] of your words give light [revelation, understanding, and application].[277]

---

271   Proverbs 25:4
272   Matthew 13:44
273   Psalm 119:15
274   Charles Bridges, *The Christian Ministry: With an Inquiry Into the Causes of Its Inefficiency*, 193
275   Psalm 106:7
276   Psalm 119:99
277   Psalm 119:130

Digging deep into the heart of God will be repaid with an incredible treasure, like striking a seam of gold or an oil reservoir. Little wonder, then, that God instructs his people to meditate on his words and it will make them prosperous and successful.[278]

Dreams and visions, enigmatic speech, and *rhema* words from God bring counsel, offering direction to our lives. These "pearls of great price" do not deserve to be trashed underfoot.[279]

Reactive or Responsive

From time to time, it is helpful to ask ourselves: "Which type of person am I: reactive or responsive?" Making progress in the realm of the Spirit requires cultivating the ability to be responsive. Reactive people tend to be impulsive, making decisions on the spur of the moment, without proper reflection and evaluation. They are swept along by the changing tides of their circumstances and ruled by their emotions. There is a story about two Christian brothers meeting up. One said to the other, "How are you?" The other replied, "Alright, I suppose, under the circumstances." To which the reply came, "What are you doing under there?" Reactive people tend to live under their circumstances and have not learned to live above them.

Jesus was responsive, not reactive. "The Son only does what he sees the Father doing."[280] Responsive decision-making is governed by waiting on the Lord, seeking his voice and looking to see what the Spirit is doing. So many mistakes are made by not following Jesus' way of enquiring of the Lord. It is about identifying the purposes of God situationally, perceiving his will, his way and his timing. To impulsive, reactive people any way and time seems good.[281] But spiritual people will step back into their spirits and seek the Lord's counsel.

For instance, when it comes to dream interpretation, remember that if God is the genuine author of a dream, then he is the only

---

278	Joshua 1:8, Psalm 1:2-3
279	Matthew 13:45, Matthew 7:6
280	John 5:19
281	John 7:6

one qualified to interpret it.[282] Otherwise, we can find ourselves beginning in the Spirit but ending up in the flesh, making all sorts of wrong assumptions as to its meaning and purpose. Remember —to assume is to make an ass of you and me! A revelation may be authentically from God but at any stage in the process of reception we can hijack it, missing God's intention for our lives. A godly dream, vision, verbal prophecy or *rhema* word from Scripture can be misinterpreted and misapplied, leaving a sour taste in everyone's mouth. Satan would be only too happy with that! Beware of selective hearing and selective interpretation. So much time and effort is wasted by turning to our own thought processes for answers. A significant key in the life of the Spirit is the practice of consulting the Lord and asking questions. We must beware of jumping to conclusions. What begins in the Spirit should be concluded in the Spirit. When we make him our Alpha and Omega, we begin with his word and end with his interpretation.

When a patient seeks to be his own consultant doctor, it will invariably lead to a wrong diagnosis and prognosis. This was a big mistake Joshua made with the Gibeonites, and the Jews had to live with the consequences of the deception for generations to come.[283]

In Joshua's time, the news of the Israelites' military successes at occupying the Promised Land became widespread. Neighbouring nations rose up to make war against Israel. The Gibeonites, however, resorted to deception.[284] They sent a delegation to the Israelites, dressed as impoverished people from a faraway land, and sought to deceive Joshua's people into making a peace treaty. God had specifically instructed Israel not to make any treaties with the locals. Joshua knew enough to consult God before acting. This time, however, God's people did not see through the deception, and, failing to seek God's guidance, they rushed ahead with their own plans. "We can handle this one on our own. No need to consult God about such a straightforward and simple matter. After all, we have made tougher decisions than

---

282 Daniel 2:27
283 Joshua 9
284 Joshua 9

this before!" But they had given an oath to protect the Gibeonites and had to keep their word, even though they eventually realised they had been tricked. The Israelites made their decision based on appearances. For generations to come, this awkward alliance would become a source of heartache to Israel.

Nothing is more exasperating to a parent than the newfound independence of a 3-year old. "Let me do it! Don't help me! I can do it myself!" This is a dependent child exercising his awakening sense of independence. The parent's help may no longer be wanted by the child, but that does not mean it is not needed! Compare the unexpected problem of the Gibeonites and Israel's immature response. What decisions are we tempted to make without referring to God? God delights in guiding those who acknowledge their need of him,[285] and the consequences of ignoring him cannot be ignored.

Snap judgments would be alright if they didn't have the habit of often coming un-snapped!

Let us try our hand at a little detective game. Think about this and then select the correct answer: A woman running breathlessly down the road is being hotly pursued by an equally breathless man, who is gaining on her at every step. Is the man (a) a criminal, (b) a bill collector, or (c) a jogger?

Correct answer: he is a jogger, and so is his wife! They are out for their morning run, and he is just about to pass her.

God's training in the school of the Spirit is intended to develop the discipline of an enquiring mind, relying upon God's wisdom and power. The Bible reveals how God took the initiative to school his servants in asking questions of him.

The speed with which God answers our questions can be staggering and we need to learn to trust the first impressions that come to us. When we are not so assured in our ability to hear God we can be easily dismissive of these first impressions, believing them to be manufactured by ourselves. We need to learn to discern the spontaneous flow of the Holy Spirit's thoughts to us. We will not always be hundred percent accurate but

---

285   Proverbs 3:5-6

making mistakes is part of the learning process if handled with humility. God has allowed for human error and he has planned for our mistakes to be made into victories if we are willing to learn from our mistakes. Remember faith is a four-letter word spelled "R.I.S.K". Nothing ventured, nothing gained. Improved discernment comes with practice and practice makes perfect. Frequency develops effectiveness.

God desires dialogue, interaction and exchange with us. His primary objective is our personal development and maturation. Everything he does and says serves this purpose. His preferred method is partnership. He is the source of all truth and wisdom, yet he nurtures and matures us by getting us to be proactive and highly responsive in the process. He often employs questions. This works on both sides. There are times when God asks us questions and there are other times when he waits for us to question him. Ask, seek, knock. Revelation is released on the basis of our asking and seeking. The counsels of God are ready to be accessed but they wait our asking. Progressive unveiling or unfolding of God's thoughts is given on the basis of seeking. We see this interaction so clearly in God's dealings with his confidants, his attentive people.

God is perfect and all-knowing. God is God! Therefore, he does not ask questions for his sake, but for ours. In the back and forth of asking questions, our Father is seeking to develop kingly qualities in his people. "To search out a matter is the glory of kings."[286] King David was praised by God as a man after his own heart. A notable feature of the king was his habit of enquiring of the Lord. It is a partnership. We learn to develop a mature spirit not by making assumptions but by seeking the Lord for the interpretation and application of his counsel to us. When we receive revelation from God without referring to him for discernment of the source, authentic interpretation and right application, we make ourselves vulnerable to false understandings. Otherwise, we can begin in the Spirit and end up in the flesh. The purpose of metaphorical language in the kingdom of God is to

---

286   Proverbs 25:1

keep us reliant upon the Lord. Spiritual maturity comes through dependency. Self-reliance will keep us soulish and immature, and will possibly create disastrous consequences for ourselves and for others.

Authentic dreams and visions from God can be highly symbolic, employing enigmatic, metaphorical language. Our job is to refer back to God and ask questions for interpretation and application. "You are showing me this, Lord, but what does it mean, and what action do I need to take?" An exceptional example of this essential practice of encounter, dialogue and exchange is to be found in the prophet Zechariah's writings.[287] Through this approach God is teaching us the value of dependency and submission, saving us from starting successfully in the Spirit but ending up wrongly in the flesh, moving away from authentic revelation to carnal assumption and presumption. Peter was severely rebuked by Jesus when he made this mistake.[288] Progressive and developmental revelation is often released on the basis of asking right questions. Doors are opened when we learn to knock. Knocking is God's method of teaching us to interact and partner with his authority and power. It can also draw out from us the creativity God has placed within us.

The spiritual discipline of asking good questions of God develops our acuteness of hearing, sensitivity to his voice, and our dependency upon his wisdom. Our spirits bond more strongly with the Spirit of God, and we are saved from a history of derailments and repetitious false assumptions. When Jesus told the apostles that Lazarus' illness would not end in death, they jumped to the wrong conclusion that Lazarus would not die. What Jesus meant was that Lazarus would die but death would not have the last word.[289]

We would do well to remember the wise counsel, "Do not confuse the gift of discernment with the gift of suspicion."

---

[287] The prophet's questions: Zechariah 1:9, 19, 21, 2:2, 4:4, 11-12, 5:6, 10, 6:4. God's questions: Zechariah 4:2, 5:2. Compare with Jeremiah 1:11-15, Amos 7:8, 8:2 and Revelation 7:13.
[288] Matthew 16:23
[289] John 11

Prayer

*Lord of unchanging power and wisdom,
continue to inspire me to wait upon you and enquire of you.
Help me to practice asking you good questions
and to reflect and dig deep into your wisdom when you ask questions of me.
Help me to abide in you and in your counsel
that I may leave behind the disempowering habit of beginning well in the Spirit
and ending badly in the flesh,
of jumping to conclusions based on human logic and reason
without consulting you,
that when I need to make decisions and take action
I will be saved from false choices
but mount up with wings as an eagle,
and in your light see light.
May I be aligned more and more with the Mind of Christ.*

9

The Wilderness School

If spirituality matters, it matters most under pressure.[290]

Friendship with God is no bed of roses, unless you include the thorns. His ways are curious, to say the least. Have you ever considered how God treated his close friends in the Bible? Those he truly took pleasure in were subjected to hardships, adversity and severe conflict. Joseph was chosen by God and given an unsurpassable call, promising to lift him up over his family, only to be thrown down into a pit and a prison. Moses was called by God to return from exile and enter Pharaoh's presence to demand the freedom of his enslaved people. That is a bit like sending the Chief Rabbi to confront Hitler in Berlin.

The Lord said that even though Moses would courageously obey God and deliver the message, God would instantly whisper into Pharaoh's ear, hardening his heart and inciting him to resist Moses' demands.[291] Curious! Is it any wonder that Moses complained to God?[292] David was promised a kingdom only to spend many years ignominiously hiding in a desert from Saul's murderous threats. There seems to be a contradiction in the way God treats his friends.

---

290 Graham Cooke, *Qualities of a Spiritual Warrior*, 101
291 Exodus 4:24, Exodus 3:19, 4:21
292 Exodus 5:22-23

It makes one wonder that if God is like that with his friends, who needs enemies?

The Example of Job
"Have you considered my servant Job?" says God to Satan, and continues, "There is no one like him on the earth, a blameless and upright man who fears God and turns away from evil."[293] God seems to be rather proud of Job. In fact, this is the most unqualified divine praise given to anyone, except Jesus, in the Bible. God considers Job to be perfect, better than Noah, Abraham, Moses or David. Proud of his friend, God wants to show off just how faithful Job is. Curiously, after boasting on his good friend, God agrees to inflict on Job a time of great pain and isolation, both physical and mental. Job's reverence of God has endeared him to God in a very deep way. He is manifestly proud of Job, yet he expressed his friendship with Job by setting him up for trouble.

Israel in the Wilderness
Obedience to God can get us into some very strange places—places that test our reason and wisdom. Following God can seem to lead us to the wrong conclusion. He can call us to go forward and then proceed to take us backward. He can call us upward and then proceed to lead us downward. When the Israelites left Egypt, the place of their enslavement, God had promised to take them north, to the Promised Land flowing with "milk and honey". Instead, against expectations, he led them south into the burning desolation of the Sinai Peninsula.

If someone promised to lead us in one direction but then proceeded to take us in the opposite direction, we would probably think the person either did not know what he was doing or he was someone who did not keep his promises. We would conclude that either he was incompetent or a liar. This is pretty much how the Israelites must have felt when they sought to obey God after escaping Egypt.

---
293   Job 1:8

God promised to take care of them, to provide and to protect, but he led them into barren and life-threatening places, devoid of food and water. Time after time, the people believed God had played them false, was not up to the job, and had deserted them. Repeatedly, God's people were led into situations that caused them to feel disappointed, betrayed and abandoned. Yet, each time, God had something truly miraculous and marvellous waiting for them.

After escaping Egypt, they were backed into a cul-de-sac, with the Egyptian army chasing behind them and the unsurpassable Red Sea in front of them. They were between the devil and the deep, blue sea, with nowhere to go. Yet, God was with them, and he opened a way where there was no way.

After the triumph of the Red Sea, they ran headlong into more life-threatening challenges of thirst and hunger. After three days without water supply they saw an oasis in the distance, but when they got there they found the waters were undrinkable. They had arrived at Marah!

More was to come. Hunger was ahead, and more thirst. Yet, God had planned each step well in advance, with solutions ready for them and provision for every need. At Marah, over many years, a tree had sprouted and grown, waiting to be used of God for this exact time of Israel's need. Quail had been blown off their migratory course to fall exactly at the right time and in the right place for God's people. God knew in advance that they would have no water and had prepared a huge underground reservoir of water, locked under a great rock, waiting for this exact time to minister to a need, which the Lord knew would arise far in the future, and for which he would have the remedy ready and waiting. God planned ahead, seeing way in advance the needs of his redeemed people. It speaks of his love, care and power at a deeper level than we can imagine. He is the same today: he plans ahead for our welfare! We are his redeemed people today and our needs have already been anticipated by our loving Father, who sees far ahead and long before. His far-seeing grace is ever for us. All he asks of us is to trust that we are always under the hand of his undeserved, unearned grace and that he is ever-ready to care for us, because that is the kind of God he is and not because we are holy enough. Israel's story in the wilderness is our story.

Trials may take us by surprise, but never him. They may catch us unprepared but never him. Left to ourselves, adversity may be more than we can bear, but we are never left to ourselves. God is never taken by surprise. He is never unprepared. He always plans ahead. He never leaves us to ourselves. God has planned the course we should take and he walks with us.

One thing God is not: predictable. Although he is consistent in who he is, he is not predictable in his ways. He will always be the same, unchanging in his love, grace and mercy, but he will never be predictable in the implementation of his wisdom for our lives. Through all the Israelites' wanderings in the desert, God accompanied them for all of the forty years! Though the wilderness can be a place of dryness and despair, it should be understood that it is also a place where God is. He drove the Israelites into the desert but he did not leave them by themselves. It was a barren wilderness with no food or water. They had to wait on God to rain down manna before they could eat. They had to depend utterly upon God to provide them with the basic necessities of life but, because God did not function according to their schedule, their sense of security was greatly threatened. From their vantage point, God did not seem to be their meal ticket after all. Against expectations, he was not the God that would make their life easy. They were disappointed in him. They felt abandoned by him. Consequently, they were tempted to abandon him. Their faith in God was severely tested. They had assumed God was predictable. The wilderness, therefore, is used by God as a place of emptying out, where we are compelled to give up on a predictable kind of a God.

In the midst of adversity that seems meaningless, even contradictory, the deep purposes of God are at work. What bothers us most when trials come our way is the sense of meaninglessness, the loss of any sense of purpose. We cannot see why this thing is happening to us. It appears so opposite to what we expect, but God is working out his purposes, just as he did with Job. All he asks is that we trust him and believe in his superior wisdom. As Job confessed, "Shall we indeed accept good from God, and shall we not accept adversity?"[294]

Jesus in the Wilderness

After the Father expressed his very deep affection and abiding pleasure in Jesus, saying, "This is my beloved Son in whom I am well pleased,"[295] he rewarded him by casting him out into the desert, isolating him from all human support, and subjected him to a threatening encounter with Satan himself. Matthew, Mark and Luke all describe Jesus' wilderness experience.[296] They tell us that the Spirit of God drove Jesus into the wilderness to be tempted by the devil. The verb "drove", *ekballo* in the Greek manuscript,[297] has a nuance of compulsion and violence. It is the same word used to describe the forcible expulsion of demons. It was the Spirit of the living God who thrust, pushed, and forcibly compelled Jesus forward into the wilderness. It was God's initiative, just as he had orchestrated the Jews going into the desert at the Exodus and permitted Satan's harrowing of Job. This was not going to be some sort of beautiful mountain retreat. The devil himself was going to hound Jesus for forty days in a desolate wilderness. This was the place where the newly baptised Jesus was violently forced to remain and where he would be compelled to encounter Satan himself. In this desert experience, Jesus would suffer from hunger, thirst and loneliness. It was there that he was tempted to desperation and to give up on God altogether. All this was orchestrated by the Father. The way of the wilderness is one of the ways of God. All who desire to follow Christ and be formed into his likeness will ultimately experience the Holy Spirit's wilderness school. Spurgeon called it "the Oxford and Cambridge for God's students."[298]

---

294   Job 2:10
295   Mark 1:11
296   Matthew 4:1, Mark 1:12, Luke 4:1
297   *Strong's Concordance*, 1544
298   Charles Spurgeon, "Marah Better Than Elim", sermon 2301, delivered 26 March 1893

What is it exactly? And why does it happen to those who are faithful to God and who earnestly desire to live their lives in harmony with his will? The Bible has much to say on this issue. Scripture often depicts God's presence or blessing as life-giving water—streams, oases and rivers.[299] On the other hand, it describes times of distress, doubt, and alienation from God as deserts and wildernesses. In the Old Testament, a wilderness is a barren and arid place, devoid of significant human life. It is a threatening place inhabited by wild animals and demonic forces: a place of wandering and restlessness. The first reference to the desert in the Bible is in Genesis, where the desert is depicted as a place of exile, inhabited by those consigned to its bleak landscape to live an outlaw and even criminal existence.[300]

However, in Exodus, the same desert environment that was so clearly associated in Genesis with desolation and violence, adds a transformative and supremely positive spiritual significance. The desert was the location chosen by God to be devoid of the influences of other peoples and their idolatrous practices. It was the place where his people would be made ownerless and stateless, like the desert.[301] God used the desolate and lonely surroundings of the Sinai desert to create an atmosphere that would be extremely conducive to an entire nation abandoning the effects of malevolent servitude in idolatrous Egypt. Instead, the separating and purifying impact of the desert was intended to inspire them to focus upon the majesty and greatness of their sovereign God and their desire to be owned by him.

In a spiritual wilderness, God feels remote, absent and unresponsive. Familiar landmarks in the Spirit are no longer available in the trackless wastes of the desert. Faith's certainties are put under great pressure, and we feel alone, vulnerable, lost and unprotected. It is the place where we are bedevilled by the fear of hopelessness and the unknown. It is the place of confrontation with Satan.

---

299 Psalm 1:3, 92:12-14, Jeremiah 17:8
300 Genesis 16:7, 21:14, 21:20-21
301 A Hebrew word for "desert" is *hefker*, and it bears connotations of being ownerless and stateless.

Peter's Sifting

The night before Jesus went to the cross, he told Simon Peter,

> Simon, behold, Satan has demanded permission to sift you like wheat; but I have prayed for you, that your faith may not fail; however, when you turn back to Me, I want you to strengthen your brothers.[302]

To sift wheat was to separate grain from the chaff, the good from the bad. When Satan sought permission to sift Peter, however, his purpose was not to get rid of what was bad in him but to destroy his faith so that nothing good was left. Without permission from God, the "accuser of the brethren" could not act. Satan could do only what the Lord allowed. Jesus' prayer limited Satan's power and scope. The Lord set the boundaries. God, in his omniscience, gave Satan permission to sift Peter because it would accomplish his own higher purposes. When Jesus said, "Satan has demanded permission to sift you like wheat", he used the plural form of you. Jesus' message was inclusive of all the disciples. God, because he is all-knowing, allows Satan to have a limited degree of influence in all our lives, just as we saw in the case of Job. Though that can be unsettling for us, we must remember that God is the Alpha and Omega, always supervising the process and having the final word.

Sifting is a way used by God to form us into the persons he redeemed us to be. He chooses to allow Satan's influence in our lives to accomplish his purposes.[303] Christians cannot be tested and tried in a way that God would be unable to use for their good and his glory. Sift-able souls are precious in God's eyes; they are like refined gold.[304] In the process of sifting, God pushes us beyond our capabilities so that we must trust him. As Job confessed, "Though he slay me, yet will I trust him."[305]

Many of us will have gone through a number of wilderness experiences in our lives: traumatic separation from a partner, a

---

302   Luke 22:31-32 NASB
303   Genesis 50:20
304   Psalm 66:10, Proverbs 17:3, Isaiah 48:10, Zechariah 13:9, Malachi 3:3, 1 Peter 1:7
305   Job 13:15 NKJV

serious illness, the death of a loved one, the suffering of a loved one, the death of a dream, failure, addiction, bankruptcy, loss of reputation or rejection by a friend. Our conversion to Christ offers no rest from the struggles of life. Like Jesus, all of us are eventually thrust into the wilderness of life.

The spiritual wilderness feels different for different people. For some, it is a place of intense and devastating loss. For others, it is associated with feelings of emptiness, weariness and listlessness. The experience can last for days or for years.

Christian spirituality seeks to describe this harrowing experience initiated by the Spirit of God with a number of metaphors: valley of shadows, dark night of the soul, God's hiddenness.

Valleys of Shadow

> Even though I walk through the valley of deep darkness I will fear no evil, for you are with me; your rod and your staff, they comfort me.[306]

> When you pass through the waters, I will be with you; and through the rivers, they shall not overwhelm you; when you walk through fire you shall not be burned, and the flame shall not consume you . . . Fear not, for I am with you.[307]

God does not promise us a pain-free life. Quite the opposite! For every mountain-top there is a valley. This is true not only in the natural world but also in the spiritual world, along the road of sanctification and formation in Christ. The Lord does not say we will be spared tribulations.[308] On the contrary, he leads us through dark valleys of fear and wildernesses of hardship. God could step in and air-lift us out of them. God could suddenly switch on all the lights and dispel the darkness, bringing rest, healing and deliverance. We love the idea of being "raptured" out of a valley of the shadow of death but the Bible also shows

---

306   Psalm 23:4 ESV. Emphasis is mine.
307   Isaiah 43:2, 5 ESV. Emphasis is mine.
308   John 16:33

us times when people were rescued by enduring and passing through the valleys. Even though David said, "You are with me", there was no immediate ending of the valley. He discovered the presence of the Good Shepherd in the darkness of the valley. There is a faith that believes for an air-lift out of the valley and then there is the journey of faith for God's presence leading us through a valley. There are times to enjoy and times to endure. Endurance produces strength. The intention of passing through the floods and fires is to make us stronger. Strength is developed through resistance.

There are times when we find ourselves in difficulties because of our own making. We are reaping what we have sown. There are times when it is appropriate to ask God, "Have I done something wrong? Is it some unconfessed sin? Are you trying to get my attention on something I'm avoiding?" There are other occasions, however, when the journey is designed by the Holy Spirit to mature and strengthen our relationship with God. It is in the darkness that our hold on God is tested and proved. There are seasons when our desire to avoid the valley and control it does not work, and then everything inside us wants to run away. Our fears kick in, and worry and doubts haunt us. This is precisely the time to dig deep into God and not run from him. We need to dig deep into who he is, dig deep into what he has said, and dig deep into what we truly believe.

Elijah was an amazing man of God. He witnessed an incredible turnaround with God bringing fire from heaven but when he learned that Jezebel sought his life, he panicked and ran over a hundred miles to escape her. He reached the desert feeling useless and worthless, in effect, asking God, "Let me die. I want out of the ministry, and out of life!"[309] Panic and running away will cause all sorts of dark thoughts to take our hearts captive. In those moments we must fight those thoughts with the truths of who God has revealed himself to be, who he wants to be for us, and who he declares we are in Christ.

---

309   1 Kings 19:4

Soul-sick with discouragement, Elijah withdrew to a cave on Mount Horeb (Sinai) for the night. His physical environment mirrored his interior darkness, his spiritual dead-end. His wilderness wandering was a time of questioning his beliefs and confidence in God. On Mount Carmel, he had confidently challenged the people with "How long will you waver between two opinions? If Yahweh is God, follow him."[310] During his flight to the wilderness, Elijah would reconsider his beliefs and even God would cross-examine him.[311] The wilderness is a place of soul-searching and self-examination. It makes us question everything we have ever learned. "How can a loving God allow this to happen to me? Does God really exist? Is he truly for me? Why doesn't he show himself? Where is he? Has he abandoned me?"

In the Bible, there are numerous references to God hiding himself, even pretending and play-acting.[312] In dark and distressing times God can seem to disappear. He can neither be seen, heard, nor felt, and our faith can seem hollow and meaningless. Yet God's objective is to draw us into a deeper, stronger faith, with less reliance upon our fickle feelings, and a deeper, more abiding intimacy with the Lord. This, after all, is God's ultimate goal for each one of us.

Elijah would come out of his dark place, revitalised with fresh vision and purpose, ready for the next chapter God would write.[313] Elijah is the classic case of how man's disappointments can be designed by God to become the place of God's appointments.

Lord, I would rather walk in the dark with you than sit in the light without you.

The great travellers on the spiritual road describe the dark valleys and arid wildernesses as places through which we must travel in order to reach a place of greater intimacy with God. In Hosea's time, God led Israel through the wilderness to allure

---

310   1 Kings 18:21
311   1 Kings 19:9, 13
312   God's hiding will be treated at greater length in the next chapter.
313   1 Kings 19:9, 15-16

the nation back to himself.[314] The road of formation in Christ is a highway of holiness,[315] where the seasons of valleys and wildernesses strip us down, purge, purify and refine us to Christ alone. Like any form of transformative discipline, it does not seem pleasant at the time.[316]

Dark Nights of the Soul

St John of the Cross, a 16th century Spanish mystic, is known for introducing us the concept of the dark night of the soul. It is an experience of spiritual emptying, purging and refining, in which comforts are stripped away to leave the soul in the presence of nothing but the invisible and silent workings of divine grace. It is called a dark night because to human experience this work of God's grace is for a time hidden from our understanding and emotions. The intellect is left cold, and the emotions are seemingly barren. It is dark to our understanding. As unnerving as it is, especially the first time, it is actually a profound experience of spiritual healing, not a loss of faith. The dark night strips away human illusions and pretensions.

There are no religious crutches for us to lean on in the desert of soul's dark nights. Past spiritual practices—worship, prayer, Bible reading, fellowship—no longer hold much comfort for us. We feel we have been exiled to a barren land, where there is no relief from the derelict landscape. Much of the time our faith feels as if we were hanging on by our fingernails. In fact, we are being trained to worship at a more elevated level—to worship more in spirit and less from soulish comforts. John of the Cross said, "Souls begin to enter into this dark night when God draws them out from being beginners." Like Elijah, the beginner is being weaned off the earthquake, wind, and fire to be able to hear the still, small, voice of God. The way to spiritual maturity leads away from an over-dependence on sensual stimuli to a purer, deeper faith and love. Worship of God that depends on an

---

314 Hosea 2:14
315 Isaiah 40:3
316 Hebrews 5:5-11

emotional high is based on an immature, shallow and vulnerable faith. Wilderness experiences purge and refine the believer's faith. As a result, when times of hard testing come, the believer is able to stand and withstand in greater strength and conviction than if he had never been "sand-blasted" in the desert experience. The way to spiritual maturity in Christ inevitably includes desert wanderings of disconcerting confusion and arid darkness but the other side of the desert brings a far deeper and richer faith. Jesus came out of his desert experience "in the power of the Spirit".[317]

Success in the wilderness comes by learning to exalt our faith above our feelings. We continually rehearse our faith in God's majestic sovereignty and love, even though our feelings are barren. There is a "though-yet" in God we need to learn if we are to climb the heights of spiritual maturity.

> "Though the mountains be shaken and the hills be removed, yet my unfailing love for you will not be shaken nor my covenant of peace be removed," says the Lord, who has compassion on you.[318]

And as Job declared, "Though You slay me, yet will I trust You."[319] For every "though", there is a "yet" in God. The wilderness experiences are designed to develop within us a yet-belief in God for every though-experience we encounter in our desert wanderings.

Genuine spirituality calls a person into a deep psychological change. This change comes from opening our hearts to love. This love, though, is not what we ordinarily think of as love. It is not about romantic sentiments. This love is not about sensuality and sexual pleasure. The giants of prayer have known that for ages. True love is a matter of seeking God more than anything else, more even than our own life. To live in true love means to do God's will, despite our feelings or lack of them.

To do God's will, therefore, is to give of ourselves through patience, tolerance, mercy, compassion and understanding, and

---

317 Luke 4:14
318 Isaiah 54:10 NIV
319 Job 13:15 NIV

not to receive personal satisfaction from the world. In fact, true love means to continue giving, even if you receive nothing but rejection and hatred in return. True love means to refuse to hate and not to wish harm to come upon others. It means to die to ourselves. Otherwise, we will be serving nothing but our own narcissistic desires. Dying to self is about loving God more than anything or anyone else in this world.

True Perspective

When we are enduring a wilderness experience, the devil will seek to turn it to his advantage. As in Jesus' case, Satan's supreme goal is to get us to draw away from God. He will seek to make us doubt the integrity of God's Word, to destroy our fellowship with God, to undermine our self-worth and to steal our destiny and blessings. It is a time when we can become confused, frustrated and irritable. Satan seeks to manipulate this season to make us disillusioned with God and seek comfort outside of God. In the wilderness we are tempted to do our own thing and try to make things happen in our own strength.

A common temptation in the wilderness season is to believe we have fallen out of favour with God, and that in some way he is angry with us, but that is not so! Believing that we are no longer the object of God's wrath and condemnation is foundational to living the redeemed life in Christ.

> Therefore, there is now no condemnation for those who are in Christ Jesus.[320]

Satan will do everything he can to get us to believe that God is disappointed with us and does not love us. The devil will attack the very cornerstone of our faith—the love of God. How did Jesus defeat the devil? His sole recourse was to submit himself fully to the Father and place all his confidence in the authority and integrity of Scripture as the Word of God. The truth of God's Word became a weapon in the hand of Jesus, defeating

---

[320]   Romans 8:1

every attack and driving Satan away. As a result, Jesus came out of his wilderness season in the power of the Holy Spirit, better equipped and built up to apply God's victories to others' lives. The knight had won his spurs through his victorious struggle against the dragon. In the wilderness, he had been tested and proved himself worthy. And now Jesus says to us, "Come, follow me."

God uses our wilderness experiences to refine us into the people he desires us to be.[321] The wilderness is a place where God has purposed to build our faith and character but that only happens when, despite all feelings to the contrary, we lean on the truth that God really loves us and loves us unconditionally. To do this, God requires us to be stripped of competing supports and comforts and live by naked faith. Devoid of emotional and mental consolations, despite feelings to the opposite, we learn to live more securely in the realm of faith than the fiction of our feelings and circumstances. In the spiritual wilderness, though we have no idea where we are and where we are going, God knows, and he is right there with us in the desert, though hidden from sight for a season.

Adversity Is Training for Reigning

The way of the Spirit is to train us in two seasons: enjoyment and endurance. When we are not in a season of enjoyment, we are in a season of endurance. In wilderness seasons, the Father's intention is to produce within us endurance, increase our faith and make us mature, so that we lack nothing in Christ. His purpose is to train champions, who stand strong and secure, expectant and assured before him, authoritative and bold before the enemy, and confident and inspirational before other people.

There is something about a faith that has been fired and hammered out on the anvil. Once we have endured a trial, something traumatic enough to shake our faith, and yet it has not destroyed our faith, we have greater confidence that the next time trouble comes God will bring us through. Once we have

---

321   Romans 8:29, Ephesians 1:5, Philippians 3:21

passed through one valley with God's help, we know that when the next valley comes God will still be there. Thanks be to God who has the power to extract the precious from the worthless and out of the bad bring something truly good and honourable!

Prayer

Here I am before You, Lord, simply,
in unadorned faith,
divested of all human comfort,
naked, in the dark night of the soul.
For, I would rather walk in the dark
with you,
than sit in the light without you.
Father, we don't always understand what you're doing,
we can't fully wrap our minds around your ways,
but our hearts cry out to you
We proclaim that no matter what we face, we trust you.
We know that your plans for us are good and filled with hope.
We know that you have the best in store for us,
even though at times our circumstances seem hard to bear.
We believe that wilderness seasons won't last forever.
"Weeping may remain for a night,
but rejoicing comes in the morning."[322]
We know that light will break through the dark
and we have confidence in you to bring us through.
Because of your power and compassion, we will come through
to the other side,
with greater perseverance, stronger faith, and deeper awareness
of your presence with us.
Thank you that you are fighting for us, and will bring us out
as gold.
In Jesus' Name.

---

[322] Psalm 30:5

10

The God Who Hides and Reveals

*Truly, you are a God who **hides** himself, O God of Israel, the Saviour.*[323]

*At that time Jesus, full of joy through the Holy Spirit, said, "I praise you, Father, Lord of heaven and earth, because you have **hidden** these things from the wise and learned, and **revealed** them to little children. Yes, Father, for this was your good pleasure."*[324]

We tend to believe that openness and transparency are essential to healthy relationships. What, then, when God expresses his friendship with us by hiding? The Bible speaks of God both revealing his presence—his manifestation—and hiding himself. Many of us have moments in our lives when God's presence and favour seem obvious, but there are also many times when God seems far away and hidden. In fact, the hiddenness of God is a common objection to his existence. The term "divine hiddenness" evokes a variety of responses: the elusiveness of God's comforting presence when we are afraid and in pain, the devastating experience of divine absence and abandonment, and even an argument against the existence of God. Many of these experiences are hard to reconcile with the biblical idea that God exists and that he is a God who is deeply concerned with our wellbeing. Accordingly, the problem of divine hiddenness has

---

323 Isaiah 45:15 ESV
324 Luke 10:21

come to rank alongside the problem of evil as one of the two most argued reasons for disbelieving in God. The absence of evidence of God constantly manifesting himself is an argument used by sceptics against his existence. But the absence of evidence is not always the evidence of absence!

The major premise is assuming that we can know exactly what it is like to be God and more specifically what it is like to reason as God. But there is no way human beings can equate with a transcendent divine nature. God is far above all human intellect and love. He is all-knowing, all-powerful and present everywhere, and we are not! With the Spirit's help we can think like God, but not as God. To think with omniscience and act with omnipotence as the eternal Creator is outside of our limited human capabilities. Imagine an ant trying to understand quantum mechanics. We cannot fill God's shoes nor can his "brain" fill our heads. As G.K. Chesterton remarks:

> The poet only asks to get his head into the heavens. It is the logician who seeks to get the heavens into his head. And it is his head that splits.[325]

The gulf between divine and human love is significant enough to cast doubt on our natural expectations about how divine love would manifest itself. God may have good reasons for his hiddenness that we just cannot fully comprehend. We cannot arrive at a full explanation apart from God's direct revelation.

In times of manifestation, when God is revealed to us in tangible ways, we can feel him; we can access him emotionally: laughing, crying, overwhelmed with joy, overawed with reverent fear. The Bible provides several examples of men and women who have been exposed to the manifest presence of God, only to be overwhelmed by his true power, majesty and glory. Jacob was so stunned by his meeting with God that he was surprised he survived at all.[326] Moses was so physically altered after meeting

---

325   G.K. Chesterton, *Orthodoxy*, Garden City, New York: Doubleday and Company 1959, 17
326   Genesis 32:30

with God that the people were "afraid to come near him".[327] Samson's parents were so terrified after meeting with God that they thought they would "surely die".[328] Isaiah was so overcome by his meeting with God that he exclaimed, "Woe is me!"[329] Each of them was immediately humbled and in awe of God. Who, when exposed to the direct presence of God, could react any differently?

God could certainly overwhelm each of us with his power and glory. He could appear to us in the kind of tangible ways sceptics often demand. Moses' encounter with the majestic awesomeness of God is most telling.

> Then Moses said, "Now show me your glory." And the Lord said, "I will cause all my goodness to pass in front of you, and I will proclaim my name, the Lord, in your presence. I will have mercy on whom I will have mercy, and I will have compassion on whom I will have compassion. But," he said, "*you cannot see my face, for no one may see me and live.*" Then the Lord said, "There is a place near me where you may stand on a rock. When my glory passes by, I will put you in a cleft in the rock and cover you with my hand until I have passed by. Then I will remove my hand and you will see my back; but my face must not be seen."[330]

The Hebrew word for "cover" employed here is *sakak*, which also means to "fence", "overshadow", "block", "screen", "shut off" and "protect."[331] Humans are mortal, and the full manifestation of the immortal, holy God would destroy us. We would blow a fuse from which we could never recover. In this amazing encounter we see another reason why God shielded the full manifestation of his presence: he would protect his friend Moses from himself. Moses was protected from God by God! "You will see my back" is a euphemism for a glimpse or the afterglow of God's passing presence. Any more than that and Moses would not have survived the encounter. Even the seraphim, the fiery

---

327   Exodus 34:29-30
328   Judges 13:22
329   Isaiah 6:5
330   Exodus 33:18-23 NIV
331   *Strong's Concordance*, 5526

angelic beings closest to God's throne, need to cover their eyes before the full glare of the thrice-holy God.[332] *There is a place near me.* God wants his friends to occupy a place near him but in order to accomplish this he has to shield us in our mortality from the full manifestation of his presence. The nearness of our God is in his hiddenness as well as in his manifested presence. "I will put you in a cleft in the rock and cover you with my hand." There is a covering, keeping and protecting love of God for us.[333]

If God wants his people to love him without being overwhelmed in this way, he would have to approach us in some form of disguise. He would have to hide his power and glory for a time. Christianity reveals this to be the case, with Jesus coming to us in profound humility, voluntarily accepting the limits of a human being and hiding the full capacity of his glory and power.

Jesus was miraculously born of a virgin, possessed inexplicable wisdom—even as a child—that shocked the educated, he exercised authority over nature, performed countless miracles, healings and exorcisms, raised people from the dead, prophesied and fulfilled prophecies, produced radical conversions, loved like only God could love, died a terrible death impaled on a cross, calling for forgiveness of his enemies, and finally rose from the dead in a glorified body that could pass through locked doors. Jesus claimed to be the one true God of the entire universe and gave the people he encountered every reason to believe it. Even so, people still firmly disbelieved, enough to execute him. Maybe God knows that a more obvious presence in the world would not be good enough for many sceptics to believe. Maybe God's hiddenness is an act of mercy. Someday God will expose us directly to his power and glory, confident that his Bride, the Church, truly loves him.

The Bible, therefore, portrays God as moving in two ways: manifestation and hiddenness.[334] They have also been described as "the conscious and unconscious presence" of God.[335] St

---

332	Isaiah 6:2
333	Exodus 34:6-7
334	Graham Cooke, *Hiddenness and Manifestation*, 10
335	RT Kendall, *The Presence of God*, 4

John of the Cross, who referred to the hiddenness of God as the dark night of the soul, called the manifestation of God the "the illuminative path". Job is a textbook example of how God's presence is sometimes manifest while other times it is hidden. There are times when he reveals himself to our conscious awareness, and there are times when he seems to hide from us. He has reasons for both. In times of manifestation, God appears to draw closer to us, while in times of hiddenness he appears to withdraw from us.

Different Reactions to God's Hidden Presence

God's hiddenness is his absence and silence, prompting responses of annoyance, anxiety, and despair. The Old Testament lamented the failure of God to show up and vindicate his people. Jesus' cry of dereliction on the cross is an experience of abandonment by God.

The Bible records a number of different reactions to God's hiddenness.

God has forgotten me: "Awake, O Lord! Why do you sleep? Rouse yourself! Do not reject us for ever. Why do you hide your face and forget our misery and oppression?"[336]

God has rejected me: "Why, Lord, do you reject me and hide your face from me?"[337]

God is angry with me: "How long, Lord? Will you hide yourself forever? How long will your wrath burn like fire?"[338]

God is punishing me for some sin: "You have hidden your face from us and have given us over to our sins."[339]

God's hiddenness provoked alarm and dismay: "How long,

---

336 Psalm 44:23-24 NIV
337 Psalm 88:14 NIV
338 Psalm 89:46 NIV
339 Isaiah 64:7 NIV. See also Job 13:24 and Isaiah 57:17.

Lord? Will you forget me for ever? How long will you hide your face from me? How long must I wrestle with my thoughts and day after day have sorrow in my heart? How long will my enemy triumph over me? Look on me and answer, Lord my God. Give light to my eyes, or I will sleep in death."[340]

When we comprehend God's ways and his purposes, our perception changes, and we adopt a different perspective. We see our circumstances from God's viewpoint and we are enabled to stand up to them with greater confidence and assurance.

Waiting on God with Expectant Hope for a Positive outcome

> *I will wait for the Lord,*
> *who is hiding his face from the descendants of Jacob.*
> *I will put my trust in him.*[341]
> *Truly you are a God who has been hiding himself,*
> *the God and Saviour of Israel.*[342]

There are many reasons given in Scripture as to why God appears to withdraw his presence. Unrepented sin as an offence against the holiness of God provoked him to hide his presence from his people.[343]

> For a brief moment I abandoned you, but with deep compassion I will bring you back.[344]

Like a young wife rejected by her husband, God abandoned his people for a brief moment, yet he sought to win them back to himself. The God we serve is holy and loving.

There are times when we need to wait, because the time for God to reveal himself and fulfil his promises is not yet. This

---

340   Psalm 13:1-3 NIV
341   Isaiah 8:17 NIV
342   Isaiah 45:15 NIV
343   Deuteronomy 32:20, Isaiah 54:8
344   Isaiah 54:8 NIV

also relates to God's delays responding to the people's prayers.[345] Other times, a season of God's hiddenness relates to tests of faith. Jesus was asleep when the disciples needed his help during a storm. It was a faith-building exercise.[346]

Contrary to our feelings of abandonment and neglect in times of hiddenness, God's Word assures us that he will never leave us nor forsake us.[347] Although God seems to move away from us, he is, in fact, constantly with us, though in a different guise. He is drawing us into a new place with his Spirit, drawing us further into him. He does not withdraw from our spirits but from our senses, to purge and refine our desires and emotions. His purpose in these seasons is to purify our faith and set it on a firmer foundation.

Hiddenness is God's preferred location, where we develop trust in God's abiding presence whether he is "visible" or not. It gives us the ability to recognise his presence when he is not tangibly present and to discern his purpose for the season.

The hidden presence of God is all about our internal development—how to live victoriously from the inside out. He seeks to develop and strengthen our trust in his Word and in his revealed nature and ways. Our feelings can lie to us, and living on them does not develop depth of character or maturity of faith. We are tempted to worship our feelings and follow the Lord for the satisfaction and feel-good factor. The roller-coaster ride of emotions will betray us, keeping us vulnerable and self-focused, loving our feelings more than God. Although we can enjoy our feelings, we are not to depend on them or build our lives on them. "Peste-costalism" and "Charis-mania" are symptoms of emotionalism and corruptions of true Spirit-filled living. Trusting in God's Word will teach us to be confident in who the Lord wants to be for us when our feelings let us down. There is a marriage between the Spirit and the Word, and what God has put together, we should not separate.

---

345   Isaiah 8:17 and Psalm 13:1-2
346   Mark 4:35-41
347   Hebrews 13:5

Hiddenness Is a Time of Building

While manifestation is a time of blessing, hiddenness is a time of building. Whatever kind of day we are having, good or bad, the Lord wants us to know what truly counts has not changed:

> I am the Lord, I do not change.[348]

He is the ever-fixed centre of our lives: "Love that alters not when alteration finds."[349] Everything may change around us, and we may be experiencing change within, but he is ever-present, constant, utterly dependable, trustworthy and reliable. Good day or bad day, the Lord wants us to know how to live in the grace of his presence and unchanging nature. One day we may feel his presence and bask in the joy of it. Another day we may not feel his presence at all, but we will maintain our confidence in his unchanging love and faithfulness toward us. Hiddenness is a time when we learn to flex our faith muscles, establishing spiritual discipline in our lives, and build consistency in our walk with the Lord.

> Once established, they prevent the enemy from invading your life and touching you, because regardless of emotions, you know how to find the presence of God; you have a constant assurance of His presence and His commitment to you.[350]

Hiddenness and Wisdom Are Close Partners

> Where then does wisdom come from? Where does understanding dwell? It is hidden from the eyes of every living thing, concealed even from the birds in the sky.[351]

> You taught me wisdom in that secret place.[352]

348	Malachi 3:6
349	William Shakespeare, Sonnet 116
350	Graham Cooke, *Hiddenness and Manifestation*, 13
351	Job 28:20-21
352	Psalm 51:6 NIV

> We do, however, speak a message of wisdom among the mature, but not the wisdom of this age or of the rulers of this age, who are coming to nothing. No, we declare God's wisdom, a mystery that has been hidden and that God destined for our glory before time began.[353]

Hiddenness is a close partner with wisdom. It teaches us the wisdom of how to know God and to walk with him. As David said, "Behold, You desire truth in the inward parts, and in the hidden part You will make me to know wisdom."[354] Hiddenness is the Spirit's training centre for processing a deep truth.

> It is the glory of God to conceal a matter but the glory of kings to search out a matter.[355]

In hiddenness, we dig deep and process the things we experienced of God in times of manifestation.

Our lifelong adventure is to learn to abide in Christ. Revival is not necessary if we are abiding in Christ. We need revival only when we have stopped practising abiding. Seasons of hiddenness are essential to upgrading our relationship with the Lord. They can be included under the counsel of "deny yourself and take up your cross". Discipline is essential in order to transition from desire to delight, from yearning to attainment, from dreaming to actualisation. Practising trust and confidence in the Lord during seasons of hiddenness provides immunity from the enemy's attacks to infiltrate and demoralise us.

Times of manifestation make everything virtually effortless for us. Basking in the sunshine on a mountain-top makes love easy, worship easy, prayer easy, and faith easy. These are times when the Lord is shouldering the bulk of the relationship and carrying us. They are pleasurable times, when God is pleasing us. But in times of hiddenness, walking through the valley of deep shadows, the arid wildernesses, bereft of much emotional comfort, we are required to apply faith. We grow more in times of hiddenness than in times of manifestation. Jesus would not

---

353   1 Corinthians 2:6-7
354   Psalm 51:6 NKJV
355   Proverbs 25:2 NKJV

allow the disciples to remain on the Mount of Transfiguration but led them back to the valley below, where hardships and contention awaited them. Hiddenness is a time of self-denial, questioning, searching, exploring, and digging deeper into God and our own soul. The journey inwards is the longest journey. Manifestation is about absorption; hiddenness is about activation.

Absence makes the heart grow fonder. God seems to withdraw, so that we will desire him more. He withdraws to draw us closer. He hides that we seek and find him at a deeper level. Like the Israelites in the Sinai desert, God seeks to woo and win us, drawing us closer with "cords of love".[356] God's hiddenness is an act of love. Far from distancing himself, he seeks to allure us, Spirit to spirit. Israel came out of the desert closer to God and more equipped in the Spirit to be inheritors and possessors of the promises of God. They went in to the desert knowing deliverance under Moses' leadership but they came out of the desert having transitioned to be possessors under Joshua's leadership.

Hiddenness teaches us focused attention and forms our will. The part our will plays in discipleship is far more significant than our feelings. Feelings can take us only so far, but our will shall take us much further in following Christ. Faith says in Gethsemane, "Your will be done, not mine." In manifestation, God pleases us. In hiddenness, we please God.

Emmaus Road

There are many occasions when Jesus deliberately withheld immediate disclosure of his identity. He was assumed to be a gardener to Mary Magdalene at the empty tomb[357] and as an unidentified spectator on the lakeshore while the disciples were fishing.[358] But the classic example of hiddenness and manifestation is the story of the two disciples' encounter with Jesus on the

---

356 Hosea 11:4
357 John 20:14-16
358 John 21:4

Emmaus road.³⁵⁹ Jesus cloaked his identity, making himself unrecognisable to his disciples. He was present but hidden from them seeing him.

One of the two disciples is named *Cleopas*. Cleopas is a Greek name, and its Semitic form is *Clopas*. Clopas is identified in John 19:25 as the husband of one of the Marys who was present at the crucifixion, and it is also the name of a brother of Joseph.³⁶⁰ If Cleopas and Clopas are the same person, then this resurrection appearance on the road to Emmaus happened to the father of Simeon, who is later head of the church in Jerusalem, according to the early church historian Eusebius. Cleopas and his friend had doubtless travelled with Jesus and had often seen him begin a meal by breaking bread. It begs the question: why, if Cleopas was closely related to Jesus by both family and discipleship, was he unable to recognise Jesus after only a couple of days' absence? Luke 24:16 says that "they were kept from recognising him". The Greek word employed is *ekratounto*, which means "compelled", "forced", "held fast", "restrained" or "prevented". The verb is in the passive voice, indicating that it was an act of God preventing them from recognising Jesus. They did not prevent themselves from recognising him; God did. The same God who caused Jesus' identity to be hidden from them would later open their eyes spiritually. "Then their eyes were opened, and they recognised him."³⁶¹ "Were opened" is *dienoichthesan* in Greek.³⁶² This again is in the passive voice: they did not open their own eyes, God did! The risen Lord cloaked his identity as a predetermined and deliberate tactic to accomplish a specific agenda in the lives of his followers. And we recall that the Lord is the same, yesterday, today and for ever! His purposes do not change. In

---

359   Luke 24:13-35
360   Eusebius of Caesarea relates in his *Church History* (Book III, chapter 11), that after the destruction of Jerusalem in 70 AD, the Christians of Jerusalem "all with one consent pronounced Symeon, the son of Clopas, of whom the Gospel also makes mention; to be worthy of the episcopal throne of that parish. He was a cousin, as they say, of the Saviour. For Hegesippus records that Clopas was a brother of Joseph."
361   Luke 24:31
362   *Strong's Concordance*, 1272

hiddenness, he makes himself unrecognisable to the familiar and predictable ways of knowing him. He is preparing us to see him in a new and deeper light and to relate to a fresh revelation of himself.

Not only did Jesus prevent his disciples from instantly recognising him, as they reached their journey's end, he gave them the impression that he would not stop but would have gone further. The verb in Greek is *prospoieo*, which means "to pretend" or "to act as if".[363] It was as if he was playing with them. God is playful. It was only when they urged him to stay with them that he consented. This pretence, or play-acting, appears also in the story of Jesus walking on the water. When he approached the disciples' endangered boat, he acted as if (*prospoieo*) he would pass them by and go further.[364] The literal translation is that "he was desirous to pass them by"—he gave them the impression he would have gone further.

We understand that miracles were used by Jesus to demonstrate that God was with him, but why was he purposely passing by the disciples when he was walking on water? As the church in the boat is struggling in the storm, rowing against a furious wind, why would the Lord think of passing them by? Again, it was only when they urged him did he consent to get in the boat with them.

In the NKJV version of the two disciples' encounter with Jesus on the Emmaus road, it says that they "constrained him". The Greek verb *parabiazomai* has the basic meaning of "do violence to" or "compel", but here is used in a figurative sense: "urge strongly", "prevail upon" or "constrain."[365] The NIV says that "they urged him strongly". And so Jesus agreed. Jesus hid his presence and acted in a surprising way in order to draw out a very strong response from his followers. He did it to persuade them to call to him.

363	*Strong's Concordance*, 4364
364	Mark 6:48
365	*Strong's Concordance*, 3849 (Luke 24:29)

To Provoke a Strong Response

With the disciples in the storm-tossed boat, Jesus came close enough on the water for his disciples to see him but did not impose himself on them. He waited for their invitation before boarding their boat. What he would do to help depended on their response. He had no intention of forcing himself upon them. If they had not wanted him, he may have passed by. In the same way, if the two disciples on the Emmaus road had not urged him to come and stay with them, he might have passed them by.

He gave the two disciples on the Emmaus road a chance to react to his words and invite him in. The tension grew. Would these disciples follow through? Would they ever learn the truth about who was walking with them, teaching them and opening their eyes to deeper truth? It seems that if they were going to learn the truth and be reconciled with Jesus, it would be because they deeply desired to know the truth. And that is exactly what happened. They invited Jesus to stay with them, so that they could continue to fellowship and learn from this "stranger". But perhaps something inside of them was telling them that he could be much more than a stranger, if they would only spend more time with him. As he broke the bread and gave it to them, the scales were finally and miraculously removed from their eyes, and they recognised that it was the risen Lord. As soon as their eyes were opened, Jesus was gone, and they were left to ponder the depth of the mysteries that had been revealed to them. Something new was burning within them.

It was their enthusiastic invitation for Jesus to stay and continue to fellowship with them that resulted in Jesus revealing himself to them.

Jesus gives us many chances to invite him in. He makes himself available to us in many ways but allows us the freedom to choose how we will live our lives. He will come to us and intervene in our lives, but only if we are willing for him to do so. How often has Jesus come by each of us and presented us with opportunities to invite him into our situations?

Hiddenness is intended to cause us to dig deeper into the mysteries of God. The Lord hides his presence for a reason

—so he can develop our internal sight and inflame our hearts with a deeper faith in him. In God's economy, hiddenness as well as open revelation play a significant part in developing his friendship with us.

Prayer

Where are you, Lord? It's dark.
Are you here in my darkness?
Your light has gone out and I cannot see you in others
or in anything around me.
Once the path before me seemed so clear
but now I no longer know what course to take.
You called me, and I followed you.
You walked by my side
and all was light and life,
but now it's night, a silent desert,
and suddenly you have disappeared.
Where are you, Lord?
Once my words seemed so effective,
but now they seem so painfully empty.
Inspiration escapes me, and I find it hard to think.
All is silent. Where are you, Lord?
The pleasure I once felt in worship now eludes me.
I no longer hear the sound of your voice.
All is an effort, slow, laborious.
I look for you but I cannot see you.
I call out to you, but you do not answer.
Your absence pains me.
I would like to run away, flee; but where can I go?
Lord, it is dark.
Are you here in the darkness with me?
Where are you, Lord?
Do you still love me?
Have you finally given up on me?
Lord, answer me. It is dark.
"I am with you always.
I will never leave you nor forsake you."
Like one who is totally blind,
I will put myself completely in your hands, Lord;
you who are absent to my feelings,
yet so close to my spirit.[366]

---

366   Adapted from *Prayers of Life*, "It's Dark", Michel Quoist

11

Perspective Is Everything

Two men looked out from prison bars, one saw mud, the other stars.[367]

Both men were in identical circumstances, but their perspectives were entirely different. One looked for beauty and found it; the other focused on ugliness and found it.

Eyes have great power; they are the windows to the soul, and they can carry the light of Christ to others.

> The lamp of the body is the eye. If your eyes are sound, you will have light for your whole body; if your eyes are bad, your whole body will be in darkness.[368]

When we set our minds on what the Spirit of God desires, our lives will change for the better.

> Those who live according to the flesh have their minds set on what the flesh desires; but those who live in accordance with the Spirit have their minds set on what the Spirit desires.[369]

---

367 "The Scales of Heaven", Frederick Langbridge (1849-1922), a British clergyman and author
368 Matthew 6:22
369 Romans 8:5 NIV

Perspective, Position, Power

When believers lose sight of God's perspective,[370] they render themselves vulnerable to failure, losing their confidence in their spiritual identity and inheritance, just as the Israelites did in Moses' time. Twelve spies returned from reconnoitring the Promised Land, which God was about to give them. All of them, except Joshua and Caleb, presented a negative report, which thoroughly disillusioned God's people, causing them to distrust God and call his integrity and capability into question.

> "We can't attack those people; they are stronger than we are." And they spread among the Israelites a bad report about the land they had explored.[371]

As a result of the people's negative response, God cancelled his promise to that generation and transferred the inheritance to their children.

To walk with God is to share his perspective, just as Joshua and Caleb did. Friendship with God means we come into agreement with everything God has to say, as Jesus emphasised, "Man shall ... live ... by every word that comes from the mouth of God."[372] There is power in agreement. There is power in alignment, with seeing how God sees. To set our minds on what the Spirit desires involves coming into alignment with God's perspectives.

> The Son does only what he sees the Father doing.[373]

Those who see what God sees are empowered to release others to see the same thing and be changed by it. The Bible tells the story of two men who stood in the same situation, a dangerous situation, but they experienced it very differently from each

---

370 *Oxford Dictionary*: Perception = the ability to see, to hear, to become aware of something through the senses. Perspective = a particular attitude toward or way of regarding something; a point of view, standpoint, position, stance, interpretation, the way we look at things.
371 Numbers 13:31-33
372 Matthew 4:4
373 John 5:19

other.[374] One saw in the Spirit and enjoyed the reality God enjoys and the other was without the Spirit's perception and was frightened. Elisha, the one who set his mind on the Spirit, saw God's heavenly army outnumbering the enemy's host. "Don't be afraid", he said to his companion. "Those who are for us are more than those who are against us." Unlike his servant trembling with fear, Elisha stood calm and confident. Possessing God's perspective will do that for us. All the servant could see was an immense enemy army coming to wipe out the two of them. The odds of survival were nil. Yet his master was smiling, as if he had already won the battle. He must have looked at his master and thought he had completely lost touch with reality. Elisha's perspective caused him to stand differently from his panicking servant. Perspective affects position—how we stand in life, how we face our circumstances. We either live above or below them. Our perspective determines our stance.

What Elisha saw empowered him to pray differently. Instead of being intimidated by the situation and praying escapist prayers, anxiously pleading, "Lord, I can't stand this. Get me out of here!" He stood authoritatively before the challenge and prayed commandingly, "Strike these people with blindness." There was power in Elisha's prayer; the Lord did what Elisha asked. First, he prayed for his junior partner to receive sight of God's reality; then he prayed for his enemies to be "hoodwinked". He had the power both to bless and to curse, to open and to close, to loose and to bind. His ability to see in the realm of the Spirit empowered one person to receive the same spiritual sight, while his enemies were denied it. Right perspective creates right positioning, and right positioning produces right praying. Seeing in the Spirit influences how we stand, and our standing affects the way we pray, and the way we pray will determine the empowering we receive. There is a direct correlation between seeing, standing and strength. How we perceive will affect how we receive. Elisha's servant, without the Spirit's perception was overcome by fear, cowering

---

374   2 Kings 6:15-18

beneath the threat, and was rendered powerless to pray with confidence.

The man of God, who saw how God saw, was empowered to release his servant to see what he saw and be changed by it.

> And Elisha prayed, "Open his eyes, Lord, so that he may see." Then the Lord opened the servant's eyes, and he looked and saw the hills full of horses and chariots of fire all around Elisha.[375]

People who possess God's perspectives are empowered to release others. What happened to the servant when his eyes were opened? How did it change him? His heart changed within him. He was transformed, from anxiety to assurance, from fear to faith. Elisha had reason not to fear. His faith rested in spiritual reality whereas his servant was limited by natural perception. The things that he saw with the physical eye dominated his thinking and placed him in the realm of fear. Once the man of God prayed, "Lord, open his eyes", his servant was able to see into the realm of the spirit. What was present all the time was now made visible to Elisha's servant.

Our ability to align ourselves with the will of God will produce breakthroughs in our lives. We become what we see.[376] Learning to master the ability to see from God's perspective is about seeing through a wholly different lens.

It's a viewpoint from a higher place and a totally different dimension. Clearly, if we are to walk with the Father in His ways, then our earthbound thinking requires serious adjustment.[377]

"O Lord, open his eyes so that he may see." Elisha did not pray for his servant to be given new eyes but that his eyes should be opened. The apostle Paul's prayer for his Christian brothers and sisters was,

---

375 2 Kings 6:17
376 2 Corinthians 3:18
377 Graham Cooke, *Manifesting Your Spirit*, 29

> I ask—ask the God of our Master, Jesus Christ, the God of glory—to make . . . your eyes focused and clear, so that you can see exactly what it is he is calling you to do.[378]

The Bible says that believers are new creations in Christ. We have been born again by the Holy Spirit, made spiritually alive and given a new identity and status before God as his adopted children. Our spiritual rebirth has given us new faculties in the Spirit, which were added to our physical senses; we possess a new heart with new ears and new eyes. We now have spiritual eyes with the capacity to see in the realm of the Spirit. Our need now is not to receive those eyes second time, but to have those eyes opened. "Lord, open his eyes so he may see." Every believer has the potential to see in the realm of the Spirit but we need to exercise this faculty to develop its effectiveness. Unless we honour our Tutor, the Holy Spirit, we will not be teachable and our spiritual sight will be myopic, as if we were looking upon a telescope's lens but fail to look through it to see to the stars beyond.

> *Teach me, my God and King,*
> *in all things thee to see,*
> *and what I do in anything*
> *to do it as for thee.*
> *A man that looks on glass,*
> *on it may stay his eye;*
> *or if he pleaseth, through it pass,*
> *and then the heaven espy.*[379]

When we see through the lens of God's perspectives, we are equipped to see beyond the natural realm into the realm of the Spirit where God dwells. To see from heaven's perspective is to open ourselves up to all that heaven has available for us on earth as it is in heaven. God's perspective is a three-way lens of hindsight, insight, and foresight. It brings the past into focus, as God views it, bringing grace and mercy to liberate

---

378 Ephesians 1:18 The Message
379 George Herbert's hymn, "Teach me, my God and King", 1633

us from the oppression of our weaknesses and failures. It brings insight into the present, releasing faith for his provision, protection and guidance. It opens foresight, sight of the future God has planned for us, releasing hope, clarity of destiny and destination, and activating faith in the present for the journey ahead.

All of Life Would Be a Sign

If we knew how to look at life through God's eyes, we should see it as innumerable tokens of the love of the Creator seeking the love of his creatures. The Father has put us in the world, not to walk through it with lowered eyes, but to search for him through things, events, people. Everything must reveal God to us.[380]

All of life would be a sign, if only we knew how to look at life as God sees it. In his love, God is always attentive to us.[381] He has conceived for our lives a unique destiny, a wonderful dream cherished in his heart from eternity to eternity, and he gives us grace to discover and live what he has planned for us. He has marked out a unique and individual path for each of us to follow. Always bending over us, he guides us to bring our destiny to fulfilment, bringing light to our path and strength for our souls. All of our lives unfold before God's eyes and no part of life should be lived without being acknowledged and freely offered to him. Our birth-right is to perceive that everything is a gift from our Father, even the smallest things, the painful things, the dark nights as well as the bright days, and that it is dependent on how we perceive and respond to them whether life is beautiful or ugly.[382]

God speaks to us through every event, even the most enigmatic and seemingly insignificant one. As his friends, we must listen to him speaking in the circumstances of our lives. We must learn to be still before him long enough to catch his intimate sharing and receive his pearls of wisdom. It is better to listen to

---

380   Michel Quoist, *Prayers of Life*, 14
381   Luke 12:6-7, 21:18
382   James 1:17

him beckoning to us in this life than enter the next with regret. Perspective saves us from drifting through life without purpose or direction.

Seeing Truth

When we are focused on the real, we will be equipped with insight to discern the false, and the enemy's tactics to steal, kill and destroy are rendered useless against us. "You will know the truth and the truth will set you free", said Jesus.[383] *Ginosko*, the Greek word for "know"[384] employed in this verse also carries the meaning "to recognise", "to understand completely", "to realise", "to perceive", or "to see". Jesus stressed the importance of possessing the ability to hear and see, having "ears to hear and eyes to see", and calling those blessed who do so.[385] He taught that being born again gives people the ability to see the kingdom of God.[386] The apostle Paul reiterated that believers born again of the Holy Spirit have access to God's plans and perspectives. They have the mind of Christ.

As it is written: "Eye has not seen, nor ear heard, nor have entered into the heart of man the things which God has prepared for those who love him". But God has, through the Spirit, let us share his secret . . . The unspiritual man simply cannot accept the matters which the Spirit deals with—they just don't make sense to him, for, after all, you must be spiritual to see spiritual things. The spiritual man, on the other hand, has an insight into the meaning of everything, though his insight may baffle the man of the world. This is because the former is sharing in God's wisdom, and "Who has known the mind of the Lord that he may instruct him?" Incredible as it may sound, we who are spiritual have the very thoughts of Christ![387]

---

383 John 8:32 NIV
384 *Strong's Concordance*, 1097
385 Matthew 13:13-16
386 John 3:3
387 1 Corinthians 2:9, 14-16 JB Phillips New Testament

The Door to God's Presence

Our perspective determines whether the entrance into the presence of God is situationally and experientially open or closed to us in the present. Entrance is voice-activated: praise and thanksgiving is the language of access into the Throne Room of heaven.

> Enter his gates with thanksgiving and his courts with praise.[388]

The attitude of gratitude is a door opener; ingratitude and self-absorption close the door. The exalted Lord said to the church in the wealthy city of Laodicea, known for its medical school that produced eye ointment,

> Buy medicine for your eyes from me so you can see, really see. Look at me. I stand at the door. I knock. If you hear me call and open the door, I'll come right in and sit down to supper with you.[389]

The door to this church was closed from the inside, by people, which effectively was excluding the life-changing presence and power of Jesus from among them. The admittance of Jesus' presence would only be achieved by the people opening the door from the inside. The Bible tells us that praise and thanksgiving are the keys which unlock the door into the presence of God. Their remedy lay in the healing of their spiritual eyes and having them opened to perceive the Spirit's viewpoint. When we set our minds on what the Spirit desires, our lives will change for the better. In God's presence we understand things that we do not understand any other way. We see the big picture, and it gives us hope.

Right Perspective Brings Hope

> David said, "Lord, where do I put my hope? My only hope is in you."[390]

---

388   Psalm 100:4
389   Revelation 3:20 The Message
390   Psalm 39:7 NLT

When our hope is in God, he exchanges discouragement with confidence, so that what we are going through can become an access point to spiritual growth. Hope gives us a sense of purpose, where we are going in life, and those who possess this perspective have goals to aim for. As Paul said, "I've got my eye on the goal . . . I'm off and running."[391]

What enabled Jesus to endure the cross was his vision of the resurrection and a church that would change the world.[392] Moses relinquished palace privileges because he foresaw the Promised Land.[393]

> "By faith . . . [Moses] endured, as seeing him who is invisible."[394]

He kept his eyes on God, not on people or circumstances. Paul said, "Having done everything . . . stand firm."[395] Moses stood firm even in his eighties, because he kept his eyes on God.

Like these great friends of God, we need to continually remind ourselves of the hope that is set before us, and it will energise our walk of faith.

> "There is nothing love cannot face; there is no limit to its faith, its hope, its endurance."[396]

God is the most self-confident, upbeat, positive, hope-filled Person we could ever meet. Every dream he has about us and our future is centred on our wellbeing and everlasting friendship with him. He is a God of love, faith and hope. His desire for us is to dwell in his irresistible love, his indomitable faith and his irrepressible hope. While faith is the language of the present, hope is the language of the future. Hope is future-focused and faith-creating. Our welfare and development is our Father's chief

---

391 Philippians 3:13-14 The Message
392 Hebrews 12:2
393 Hebrews 11:24-27
394 Hebrews 11:27 NKJV
395 Ephesians 6:13
396 1 Corinthians 13:7 NEB

concern. He is totally aware of all things, not just what we are currently going through, but he also knows what is coming down the road tomorrow. He has both perfect insight and foresight and he has provided for every circumstance. This is what David meant when he said, "Those who look to the Lord are radiant." A proverb says, "For the Lord will be your confidence and will keep your foot from being caught in a trap." David said: "I would have despaired unless I had believed to see the goodness of the Lord in the land of the living."[397]

Hope means that whatever our circumstance we have a confident expectation that we will experience God's goodness. Right perspective produces positive expectations. Our Father knows the way ahead of us better than we do. He also knows the enemy's pre-planned traps and he has strategically planned to provide for us in every situation.

> I know the plans I have for you, plans to prosper you and not to harm you, plans to give you a future and a hope.[398]
>
> We know that in all things work together for good to those who love God and are called according to His purpose.[399]
>
> He who did not spare his own Son, but delivered him up for us all, how shall he not with him also freely give us all things.[400]
>
> For no matter how many promises God has made, they are "Yes" in Christ. And so through him the "Amen" is spoken by us to the glory of God.[401]

Friendship with God means that for every problem God will have a promise for a provision. He calls us to stand in our problems, holding onto his promises, and be expectant that his provision will be released.

397	Psalm 34:5, Proverbs 3:26, Psalm 27:13
398	Jeremiah 29:11
399	Romans 8:28
400	Romans 8:32
401	2 Corinthians 1:20

> For we know that in all things God works for the good of those who love him, who have been called according to his purpose.[402]

How we stand up to life, what position we hold, is affected by our perspective. As God's friends, we need to position ourselves correctly before him. Our Father wants us to see our circumstances from his perspective. He seeks to liberate us from the control of our circumstances and allow him to be in control. It is a matter of fold or focus: we either fold and live under our circumstances, or we focus on God's sovereign love and live above our circumstances. When we have God's perspective, we will stand differently. We will occupy a different position before God, our enemy, and others. We will stand before God expectantly, we will stand before the enemy confidently, and we will stand before other people inspirationally. When we stand on God's promises, courage and authority flow to us.

> Therefore take heart, men, for I believe God that it will be just as it was told me.[403]

God will show us what the enemy does not want us to see; he will give us discernment. The Lord will allow us to be seen as he sees us, not as the enemy wants us to be seen. He will show us favour. The Lord will show us practical ways to respond. He will give us his wisdom. And he will release what has been held back by the enemy. He will bring justice.

Like Elisha and his servant, God wants us to see the realities that the world cannot see. The Lord has so much more for us to see but we need to have our eyes opened to see these spiritual realities. In the midst of the trials of life, we can have our eyes opened and see God's plans and protection.

Can you imagine if God opened your eyes and you could see in situations you face the majestic, sovereign power of heaven all around you, as Elisha and his servant did? Can you imagine

---

402   Romans 8:28 NIV
403   Acts 27:25 NKJV

what difference it would make to your life if you could clearly see life from God's perspective?

Prayer

*Lord, open our eyes to see
how heaven touches and impacts this world.
Help us to perceive and abide in the assurance that
"those who are for us are more"—
the great cloud of witnesses standing in the place of power
and the mighty host of angelic warriors
are directing your kingdom
and strengthening every struggling follower on earth.
Give us heaven's perspective on this life.
Help us not to be distracted or intimidated
by the things of this world
but constantly to turn our gaze toward you
and see how you see.
Help us to have your perspective
and to perceive with clear eyes your realities
both in the hardships and in the blessings of our lives.
Lord, when we are tempted to be fearful in hardships,
remind us that you never let us go through trouble
without opening a way to your goodness, peace and love.
As we reflect on our blessings, help us to stand differently:
to stand before you expectantly,
to stand before the enemy confidently,
and to stand before other people inspirationally.*

12

Beyond the Last Mountain

I like the mountains because they make me feel small. They help me sort out what's important in life.[404]

Mountains

As a young man, I used to enjoy mountain-walking. The ascent could be arduous and the climate changeable but the rewards made the climb worth it. There was the satisfaction of having successfully navigated the slippery scree slopes, the hazardous bends and the heart-pumping steep inclines. Yet, above all, was the breathtaking wonder of finally reaching the summit, standing on a rock ledge under a bright sky and feeling the joy of the panoramic view of the valleys and mountain-range stretched out before me! All the tiredness and aching muscles of the climb were worth it because of the surpassing view from the mountain-top. Lifted high above the level of human sounds and far from human habitations, wrapped in the solitary quietness of the moment, I experienced the elation of feeling exceedingly small but joyously close to the immensity of God. The encounters kept me continuously wanting to know more, feel more, see more.

> People ask me, "What is the use of climbing Mount Everest?" and my answer must at once be, "It is of no use." If you cannot understand

---

404   Mark Obmascik, *Halfway to Heaven*

that there is something in man which responds to the challenge of this mountain and goes out to meet it, that the struggle is the struggle of life itself upward and forever upward, then you won't see why we go. What we get from this adventure is just sheer joy. And joy is, after all, the end of life.[405]

In human history, mountains have represented high points, vantage points, ascendancy and revelation in the spiritual life, places of communion with the gods or God. From the dawn of civilisation, people have either sought mountains or made facsimiles—ziggurats, the tower of Babel, pyramids—in order to reach or touch the divine. Mountains have always played a significant part in the Bible's unfolding story. Noah's ark landed on Mount Ararat, Abraham's sacrifice of Isaac took place on Mount Moriah, the law was given to Moses on Mount Sinai (Horeb), Moses viewed the Promised Land from Mount Nebo, Jerusalem's temple was built on Mount Zion, Elijah's revival fire fell on Mount Carmel, Jesus taught the Sermon on the Mount, he was transfigured in glory on a mountain, he wrestled with temptation on the Mount of Olives, he died on mount Golgotha, and he ascended into heaven from a mountain in Galilee.[406] The "mountain of the Lord" is a major feature in prophecies of the last days,[407] the heavenly Jerusalem is described as Mount Zion,[408] and it is depicted as the ultimate vantage point in heaven. We could ask, "What, then, lies beyond the last mountain?" On this last mountain the most compelling adventure of our lives will come to an end. There will be only one last thing remaining to experience: all the saints of God will be rapturously drawn into the majestic, beatific vision of God himself, paradise restored.[409]

---

405   Otis Chandler Goodreads: Climbing Everest Quotes/http:goodreads.com/works/quotes/10228518-climbing-everest-the-complete-writings-of-george-mallory (March 2013)
406   Matthew 28:16
407   Isaiah 2:2, 27:13, 56:7, 66:20, Micah 4:7
408   Hebrews 12:22
409   Revelation 14:1, 21:10, 22:3

Looking Forward

There will come a time when my links with earth will grow weaker, when my powers fail, when I must bid farewell to dear ones still rooted in this life with their tasks to fulfil and their loved ones to care for, when I must detach myself from the loveliest things and begin the lonely journey. Then I shall hear the voice of my beloved Christ, saying "It is I, be not afraid". So with my hand in his, from the dark valley I shall see the shining City of God and climb with quiet trusting steps and be met by the Father of souls and clasped in the everlasting arms.[410]

> *The mountains she has climbed.*
> *She's never failed, not once!*
> *She remembers every time.*
> *But then she sees this one,*
> *"It's far too hard for me!"*
> *Fear whispers in her ear,*
> *lies far too loud to ignore*
> *. . . That was the last mountain,*
> *she's done . . . she's free*
> *. . . but it's not her last.*
> *She's rising up,*
> *because she's done with the past.*
> *She's reached her victory,*
> *the last of the struggle is gone.*
> *Now He takes her closer,*
> *and says: "Let's go beyond."* [411]

The scenes of Revelation bring us beyond the "last mountain" of death and the world's end to Paradise itself. The triumph of Jesus will be revealed in all its splendour, where "the old has passed away . . . and the new has come."[412] C.S. Lewis has done justice to drawing out the great mystery that lies before each and every one of us:

> The things that began to happen after that were so great and beautiful that I cannot write them. And for us this is the end of all stories, and

---

410 George Appleton, *Journey For A Soul*, 241
411 Larxene Addesso, "Last Mountain", 21 April 2010
412 2 Corinthians 5:17

we can most truly say that they all lived happily ever after. But for them it was only the beginning of the real story. All their life in this world and all their adventures in Narnia had only been the cover and the title page: now at last they were beginning Chapter One of the Great Story which no one on earth has read: which goes on for ever: in which every chapter is better than the one before.[413]

Beyond this life's last mountain—death—there is no hope and no faith. There is no need for either of them, because what is believed and hoped for here is a reality there. There is no healing there. Suffering no longer exists. There is no mourning there. Death has been vanquished and all are made gloriously alive. There is no poverty, injustice or want there. All is righteousness, peace and joy in the Holy Spirit. "Behold," says the triumphant Lord, "I make all things new!"[414]

Future Perspective

From humankind's perspective, the future is unknown. It is yet to be written. Only the past and the present are knowable to us, but the eternal God lives outside the limitations of time and space and all of time is open to him. The future is as open to him as the present is to us. The future is known to him, precisely because he has already written it. He knows the end from the beginning. All times and seasons are in his hands. He is the Lord of history, past, present and future. He brings predictive prophecies to us precisely because he is the Author of the future. Like a playwright, the whole drama is known to him, the last act as well as the first. He is the Omega God—the last word, the epilogue, as well as the Alpha, the prologue.

He knows the future, not simply because he has perfect foresight, but because he is the future. Just as the resurrection is an "I am"—a person—so too is the future an Omega event. Jesus says, "I am the Omega." Jesus does not say "I am the Alpha and I will be the Omega." He says "I am the Omega" (present tense continuous). Omega is not merely an event (a final

---

413   C.S. Lewis, *The Last Battle*, Lions 1984, 165
414   Revelation 21:5

action of God), or a day (the last day of God); it is the Person of Jesus Christ himself. All of life is an adventure to the great becoming—a becoming into God, as partakers of the divine nature.[415] He is the great mystery, but he is the mystery of love. The future is a mystery to us, but there is one solid fact we do possess: it is where our Incarnate God is, and we shall be with him. Our future is the future of God. God is love and the future, therefore, is indwelt with love.

We are all born with an intuitive sense that there is something greater than this life on earth.

> He has also set eternity in our hearts.[416]

Our eternal future lies with God in an endless dynamic of joy, filled with a beauty we can only begin to imagine.

> You have made known to me the path of life; you will fill me with joy in your presence, with eternal pleasures at your right hand.[417]

Our eternal destiny is reality itself—the reality of Christ. We shall be like him.

> Dear friends, now we are children of God [present identity], and we have not yet been shown what we will be in the future. But we know that when Christ comes again, we will be like him, because we will see him as he really is [future destiny].[418]

We do not become gods but we shall be new persons where, in our hearts and character, we will be completely like him.

> And now, all glory to God, who is able to keep you from stumbling, and who bring you into his glorious presence innocent of sin and with great joy.[419]

415	2 Peter 1:4
416	Ecclesiastes 3:11 NIV
417	Psalm 16:11 NIV
418	1 John 3:2 NCV
419	Jude 1:24 NLT

Like the risen and glorified Lord, we will have a glorified body, liberated from all earthly limitation. We shall be immortal, "so that what is mortal shall be swallowed up by life."[420]

The Scriptures liken the future to a great birth, with the present as birth pains heralding a new age.[421] The future is the full and complete revelation of the beauty and glory of God united with his creation, wonderfully liberated, metamorphosed and elevated to the state of perfection in union with Christ. The future brings an inheritance.[422] God himself is the inheritance of his children,[423] when he shall be all in all.[424] The impartation of the Holy Spirit is the first fruit guaranteeing the certainty of the harvest ahead. "What we shall be has not yet been revealed", yet we shall see it, share it, and be transformed by it.[425] The Omega Day is not merely "the last day", the end, but a new Alpha, a new beginning. The last day is only the last day because it closes the door on life as it is now but it opens a new one onto a better life—the best life, where hatred and division will not have the last word and the human heart will be healed of its desperation and loneliness. God has an unstoppable end-time plan and he knows how it will take place. He has the future in plain sight. One day all creation will be liberated and transformed. The future with God is unimaginably glorious. God has promised.

This goal should change everything about our lives. It is a future destiny we can be certain we will reach. It lies beyond the last mountain—death. There is no greater truth to build our lives on and to motivate us to genuine significance than this goal. The apostle Paul, who had a tremendous impact upon this world, said,

> I strain to reach the end of the race and receive the prize for which God, through Christ Jesus, is calling us up to heaven.[426]

420	1 Corinthians 15:53, 2 Corinthians 5:4
421	Romans 8:19-21
422	Romans 8:17, 23
423	Psalm 73:25 cf. Lamentations 3:24
424	1 Corinthians 15:28
425	2 Thessalonians 1:10
426	1 John 3:2 NCV

He compared life to a race with the victorious runner looking ahead to the finish line. The finish line gives a runner clear direction, the certainty of where he is headed, and where the prize is to be found.

It is reported that a Gallup Poll claims 91% of American Christians believe in the afterlife, and that they will spend eternity in a glorious place, but most do not talk about it.[427] Bizarrely, they act as if it does not matter. It has also been said that most people today, when confronted with the thought of their own death, their primary concern is to die pain-free, whereas, previous generations' primary concern was being in a fit state to meet their Maker. C.S. Lewis wrote,

> If you read history, you will find that the Christians who did most for the present world were those who thought most of the next . . . It is because Christians have largely ceased to think of the other world that they have become so ineffective in this one.[428]

Being future-present minded is essential to being effective in the realities of here-and-now. One-dimensional thinking will severely limit the impact of our lives and the strength to endure the hardships and trials we face on a regular basis. Future-present thinking brings eternal perspective and releases hope, confidence, and endurance for daily living.

Future-present Perspective

There are *two types of people*: present people and future people —people who live just for the moment and others who look beyond, ahead, and their outlook in the present is coloured by their future orientation. Present people are preoccupied with the here-and-now and focused on present needs. But God dwells in the tension between the present and the future. Walking with God requires us to be people who walk in both the present and the future or, more correctly, people who live in the present from the perspective of the future—in other words, a prophetic

---

427   Philip Yancey, Heaven Can't Wait, *Christianity Today*, 7th September 1984
428   C.S. Lewis, *Mere Christianity*, Westwood NJ: Barbour 1952, 113

people. The worst that could be written on a Christian's tombstone is, "Here lies the body of John Smith, who left this world not knowing why he came into it!" Living future-present saves us from drifting, living aimless lives. Living future-present gives purpose, direction, movement and development. We are all on a journey toward God. Friendship with God means that the future speaks to us about hope, inheritance, fulfilment and consummation. Like an athlete in a race who keeps his eyes fixed on the finishing line, so we are to keep our eyes on the future God has planned for us and to enable it to influence how we respond to the adventure of this present life.

Our future is quite simply to be transformed into the likeness of Jesus. With this in mind, God acts in our present to move us forward into our destiny. His intention is not that we should stand still. Constant change is here to stay.

Forgetting what is behind and straining toward what is ahead, I press on toward the goal to win the prize for which God has called me heavenward in Christ Jesus.[429]

The present call is to press on into bigger things in Christ for our continued personal development. We must possess the compulsion to pursue the adventure of discovering and embracing the fullness of God's promises to us. We then take the necessary steps to believe and become the persons God envisions for us. Being future-present minded gives us more to aim for and empowers us to become more like Jesus. Spiritual progress requires continuous transition.[430]

Destiny and Inheritance

At the heart of all God's dealings with us is the issue of our inheritance in Christ.[431] Our future is connected to our inheritance; identity, destiny, and inheritance are inter-connected. We will share in the glorious inheritance of God's Son, Jesus Christ.

---

429   Philippians 3:13-14
430   Luke 9:23 NIV says "daily"
431   Romans 8:17, 23, Psalm 73:25, 1 Corinthians 15:28, 1 John 3:2, 2 Thessalonians 1:10

> Now if we are children, then we are heirs—heirs of God and co-heirs with Christ, if indeed we share in his sufferings in order that we may also share in his glory.[432]

We will be like Jesus. There will be no more sin, sickness or death. Our bodies will be immortal. Every need will be met. And we will be fully known and fully loved by God.[433] We are the Beloved of the Father, the Bride of Christ, the Temple of the Holy Spirit. We are called to inherit. We are the people of promise. To inherit we need two priceless things: faith and patience.[434] Faith is not only a gift to be received but also a confidence we need to cultivate through disciplined practice. God does not intend faith to be static; we are to learn how to increase in it. This requires patience, perseverance, and God has chosen a path for us to develop greater confidence.

We need to own our destiny and then ask ourselves how we should change in the present because of it. In the Bible, Joseph acted like a princely steward long before he was raised to the palace. David acted like a king long before he was crowned. Jesus acted like the Saviour long before he went on the cross. Our future destiny is real and alive now in God's heart and it should live in our hearts too. In the present we live as if the future was already true. We become the truth by abiding in it.

"As a man thinks within himself so he is", says a proverb.[435] What we behold we become. As we focus on our eternal future, our present takes on that reality. As we behold Jesus, we become like him. There is the famous story of St John Vianney (the Cure d'Ars), whose habit was to sit at the back of the church, and when asked, "What are you doing all day with this?" he answered, "Nothing. I just look at him and he looks at me." He knew the beauty of true friendship—just to be with the Beloved was all he asked. This enabled him to see everything in a different light, and so he wrote, "In prayer well made, troubles vanish like snow in the rays of the sun." It is our "good looks" that make us great

---

432 Romans 8:17 NIV
433 1 Corinthians 13:12
434 Hebrews 6:12
435 Proverbs 23:7

—our good looks at Jesus! Who we are today is defined by who God has decided we shall be tomorrow. Our destiny defines our identity. A person is a crown prince today because he is expected to be the sovereign king tomorrow. Rights and privileges are his today, because of who he will become tomorrow. Destiny is all!

> "For I know the plans I have for you," declares the Lord, "plans to prosper you and not to harm you, plans to give you hope and a future."[436]

God has already planned long-term for his creation. The end of history is already written. Whatever God's plans are, they are a done deal. He saw the end from the beginning. The Omega Author of the cosmos works in the present to bring us into that ultimate future.

I know the plans I have for you, plans to prosper you.

God gets great pleasure in planning our lives. He delights in seeing us led by his Spirit.

The Lord directs the steps of the godly. He delights in every detail of their lives.[437]

He loves to have a goal for us to aim at in our relationship with him. As a parent will plan an inheritance for his children, our heavenly Father has planned a glorious inheritance for us.[438] His inheritance connects with our incontestable identity, destiny and calling in Jesus. Everything he has planned for us and reserved for that last day determines his actions and brings that inheritance into our present relationship with him.

We are called to live today in the knowledge of a planned future, looking ahead to where the Lord is taking us. For our friendship with him to thrive we must be forward-thinking as he is. People who consciously focus on a planned future and aim to reach it by the way they conduct themselves in the present usually lead successful lives. But how many of our graveyards are full of unrealised, buried potential of those who lived only

---

436   Jeremiah 29:11 NIV
437   Psalm 37:23 NLT
438   John 14:2

for their today with no thought for their tomorrow? Productive Christians possess future-present mentality. The more we reflect on who God has made us to be in Christ and what we shall become beyond the last mountain, the more our thinking, believing, praying, speaking and acting will be affected by the mind of Christ in the here-and-now. It is about practising our identity and God's favour attached to it.

Paul tells us that the whole cosmic order is eagerly awaiting "the manifestation of the sons of God" and their "glorious freedom".[439]

"Everything is moving toward the fullest glory of God in us and through us. And between the foundation of grace and the goal of glory, there is the power of grace daily arriving in our lives", wrote John Piper. Because Jesus' death and resurrection is all-sufficient and all-providing, God's grace is ever flowing into "the present from the inexhaustible river of grace coming to us from the future . . . We live by faith in the ever-arriving power of future grace."[440] God has given us guaranteed assurances of this future grace, and they are intended to inspire us for how we walk with him by faith in the present. The Word of God promises that the good work he has begun in us he will bring to completion in Christ.[441] If we are going to become effective and productive disciples today and grow toward spiritual maturity, we must learn to live in the future-present. We have a God who knows our future and tells us how to align ourselves with him to create a pathway from now to then and there.[442] Our Father plans both our final destination and our journey of transformation to it. He not only sets our destiny he also desires to journey with us.

I am with you always, to the very end.[443]

It is vital that we cooperate with that journey.

---

439   Romans 8:19-21
440   John Piper, "Living by Faith in Future Grace", www.desiringgod.org, November 17 2012
441   Philippians 1:6
442   Graham Cooke, *Prophetic Wisdom*, 100
443   Matthew 28:20

Closing the Gap

When the Lord visited Abraham and Sarah, promising they would have a son of their own within a year, Sarah fell about laughing in disbelief. God responded by asking,

> Shall I hide from Abraham what I am about to do? Abraham will surely become a great and powerful nation, and all nations on earth will be blessed through him.[444]

God was making clear that he makes unchangeable plans for our future. They are a done deal in his own mind. He took Abraham into his confidence about the present because of what he saw Abraham would become in the future. God relates to us from two perspectives, which are inextricably bound together: our present identity and our future destiny. The Holy Spirit's task is to close the gap we have allowed between an insufficient comprehension of our present identity and our future destiny.

Whether it is building a new school or starting a new business, with any great venture worthy of our energies, we start with a finished product or goal in mind and then work backwards. We formulate a development plan and work out the action to implement in the present. The entire record of Scripture testifies that God's plans work on the same basis. He has "a day", a date, in mind, for fulfilment and an order of sequence to accomplish his promises. A process of change and adaptation is put into in motion to bring our hearts and minds into alignment with his will. If, however, we fail to respond positively to his ways, then the time of fulfilment can be delayed. Continuous non-compliance can lead to indefinite postponement and even cancellation, as was the case with the first generation of Israelites in Moses's time.[445] We must reach out for our future and press toward it.[446] We need to rise up and take possession of our inheritance; it awaits our rising up and taking possession of it. As Jesus said,

---

444   Genesis 18:17-18 NIV
445   Numbers 14
446   Philippians 3:12-17

"The Kingdom of God is forcefully advancing and forceful men lay hold of it."[447]

When the forces of apathy and indifference seek to enslave us, the Holy Spirit's way to freedom will prompt us to experience divine dissatisfaction. He will threaten our status quo, causing us to feel discontented and desirous for better things. The false peace of our present comfort zone will appear to us a constricting and restraining prison. It will no longer feel like the cosy cushion it used to be. A mother eagle will pull the nest from under the feet of her chicks, compelling them to explore the use of their potential to fly. The Holy Spirit moves us into a new reality.

> They will soar on wings like eagles; they will run and not grow weary, they will walk and not be faint.[448]

> You yourselves have seen what I did to the Egyptians, and how I bore you on eagles' wings and brought you to myself.[449]

We need to ask ourselves: "What has God planned for me to become in the future, and what changes do I need to make in the present? What is the difference between where I am now and where I need to go? How must I close the gap, and what changes need to take place in my relationship with God?"

In what way would we like the truth of our future destiny to have greater impact on our lives in the present? What changes do we need to make? Change requires adopting a series of transformational steps that take us from where we are now to where God desires us to be. If we are to make continuous progress, it is imperative that we become welcoming of divine dissatisfaction with our status quo. We have to possess a longing for more of God, hunger for the presence of Jesus, and a greater desire for the Holy Spirit in our lives. Because our identity in Christ is connected with an incomparable destiny and inheritance, we have to be committed to our personal development and growth. God's destiny for us will never change.

---

447   Luke 16:16
448   Isaiah 40:31
449   Exodus 19:4 ESV

Nothing can ever separate us from his love. Our salvation is safe and secure in heaven, where nothing can destroy it. Even so, God's ways can sometimes feel strange, so we need to learn how to interpret the signals correctly, being on our guard against allowing divine dissatisfaction to become disillusionment. One is constructive and growth-enhancing; the other is destructive and growth-inhibiting. Adventuring with God is like a treasure hunt —we need to ask good questions. On the day of Pentecost, two questions were asked: "What does this mean?" and "What must we do?" We need to ask the Holy Spirit what experiences we must receive to empower us to become more like Jesus.

Running the Race

God is always future-present minded. Everything he does in the present is shaped by what he has planned for the future. He is like a sprinter in a race who, springing from the starting blocks, keeps his eyes on the finish line. The apostle Paul understood this.[450] We should not let anything take our eyes off the goal— the future which God has prepared for us. We must live in the tension of what we are and what we shall be, moving forward in a life of cooperating faith. Scripture repeatedly instructs us to shift our focus from present-only mindedness to God's perspective of future-present thinking.

The future God has planned for his friends must turn our attention to the ways he employs to renew and transform us for our future state with him. Such focus will compel us to cooperate with his current assignment in our lives and the season of the Spirit he has predetermined for us. It is imperative that we learn how God thinks, how he likes to work, and we must learn how to respond willingly to the adventures he sets before us. This is the path of wisdom. If our focus is the finish line, we will be highly motivated to cooperate with the Lord in the ways he desires to fit us for eternity with Christ.

Friendship with God means change is here to stay. He calls us to accept, adjust, and arrive.

---

[450] Philippians 3:13-14

*Now to him who is able to keep you from stumbling
and to present you blameless before the presence of his glory
with great joy,
to the only God, our Saviour, through Jesus Christ our Lord,
be glory, majesty, dominion, and authority,
before all time and now and forever. Amen.*[451]

---

451   Jude 24-25 ESV

References

1. Christ in You
A.C. Spearing, Elizabeth Spearing, Julian of Norwich (author), *Revelations of Divine Love*, Penguin Classics Paperback 1998
John Stott, *Life in Christ*, Kingsway Publications Ltd 1991

2. The Bridegroom God
Francis Thompson, *The Kingdom of God*, Luath Press Ltd 1997
George Herbert, *The Complete English Poems*, Penguin Classics Paperback 1992
Palgrave, FT, *Palgrave's Golden Treasury*, Collins Classics 1968

3. Called by Love
Carl Sandburg, American Pulitzer prize-winning poet, 1878–1967
Os Guinness, *The Call*, Thomas Nelson 2003
A. Spearing (Editor, Translator), Anonymous Author, *The Cloud of Unknowing and Other Works*, Penguin Classics Paperback 2001
C.S. Lewis, *The Weight of Glory*, William Collins 2013

5. The School of the Spirit
Monty Don, *Down to Earth*, Dorling Kindersley Ltd 2017

The New Strong's Exhaustive Concordance of the Bible, Thomas Nelson Publishers 1990

Kenneth E Bailey, *Jesus Through Middle Eastern Eyes*, SPCK 2008

5. Wrestled by God

Frederick Buechner, *The Magnificent Defeat*, Harper One 1985

Joyce G Baldwin, *The Message of Genesis 12-50*, BST Inter-Varsity Press 1986

C.S. Lewis, *The Lion, the Witch and the Wardrobe*, Lions 1981

TS Eliot, *Four Quartets*, Faber & Faber 2001

John Calvin, *A Commentary on Genesis*, Banner of Truth Trust 1965

6. The Way of Silence and Stillness

TS Eliot, 'Ash Wednesday', Stanza 5, from *Collected Poems*, Faber & Faber Limited 1963

Dietrich Bonhoeffer, *Life Together*, Harper Collins 1978

Michel Quoist, *Prayers of Life*, Gill and MacMillan Dublin 1969

7. Asking Good Questions

Steve Ogne & Tim Roehl, *TransforMissional Coaching*, B & H Publishing Group Nashville 2008

8. The Wilderness School

Jamie Buckingham, *The Journey to Spiritual Maturity*, Crossover Publications Inc. 1985

Graham Cooke, *Qualities of a Spiritual Warrior*, Brilliant Book House LLC 2010

Charles Spurgeon, "Marah Better Than Elim", sermon 2301, delivered 26th March 1893

John Piper, *The Pleasures of God*, Mentor Imprint 2013

9. The God Who Hides and Reveals
Graham Cooke, *Manifestation and Hiddenness*, Sovereign World Ltd 2003
RT Kendall, *The Presence of God*, Charisma House 2017
Eusebius (Author), G.A. Williamson (Author), *The History of the Church*, Penguin Classics Paperback 1989

10. Perspective is Everything
Frederick Langbridge, *The Scales of Heaven*, Cornell University Library 2009
Oxford Dictionary, Oxford University Press USA 2012
Graham Cooke, *Manifesting Your Spirit*, Brilliant Book House LLC 2010

11. Beyond the Last Mountain
Mark Obmascik, *Halfway to Heaven*, Atria Books 2010
George Mallory, *Climbing Everest: The Complete Writings of George Mallory*, Gibson Square Books Ltd; UK ed. edition 2013
George Appleton, *Journey For A Soul*, Fontana Books 1974
Larxene Addesso, 'Last Mountain', 21st April 2010
Paul Beasley-Murray, *The Message of the Resurrection*, BST Inter-Varsity Press 2000
Peter Lewis, *The Message of the Living God*, BST Inter-Varsity Press 2000
C.S. Lewis, *The Last Battle*, The Bodley Head 1956
C.S. Lewis, *Mere Christianity*, Westwood NJ: Barbour 1952
John Piper, 'Living by Faith in Future Grace', www.desiringgod.org, November 17 2012
Graham Cooke, *Prophetic Wisdom*, Brilliant Book House 2010
Kenneth E Bailey, *Paul Through Mediterranean Eyes*, SPCK 2011

Authors in Alphabetical Order

Addesso, Larxene, 'Last Mountain', 21st April 2010
Appleton, George, *Journey For A Soul*, Fontana Books 1974
Bailey, Kenneth E, *Paul Through Mediterranean Eyes*, SPCK 2011
Bailey, Kenneth E, *Jesus Through Middle Eastern Eyes*, SPCK 2008
Baldwin, Joyce G, *The Message of Genesis 12-50*, BST Inter-Varsity Press 1986
Beasley-Murray, Paul, *The Message of the Resurrection*, BST Inter-Varsity Press 2000
Bonhoeffer, Dietrich, *Life Together*, Harper Collins 1978
Buckingham, Jamie, *The Journey to Spiritual Maturity*, Crossover Publications Inc. 1985
Buechner, Frederick, *The Magnificent Defeat*, Harper One 1985
Calvin, John, *A Commentary on Genesis*, Banner of Truth Trust 1965
Cooke, Graham, *Hiddenness and Manifestation*, Sovereign World 2003
Cooke, Graham, *Manifesting Your Spirit*, Brilliant Book House LLC 2010
Cooke, Graham, *Prophetic Wisdom*, Brilliant Book House 2010
Cooke, Graham, *Qualities of a Spiritual Warrior*, Brilliant Book House LLC 2010
Don, Monty, *Down to Earth*, Dorling Kindersley Ltd 2017

Eliot, T.S., 'Ash Wednesday', Stanza 5, from *Collected Poems*, Faber & Faber Limited 1963

Eliot, T.S., *Four Quartets*, Faber & Faber 2001

Eusebius (Author), G.A. Williamson (Author), *The History of the Church*, Penguin Classics Paperback 1989

Herbert, George, *The Complete English Poems*, Penguin Classics Paperback 1992

Kendall, R.T., *The Presence of God*, Charisma House 2017

Langbridge, Frederick, *The Scales of Heaven*, Cornell University Library 2009

Lewis, C.S., *Mere Christianity*, Westwood NJ: Barbour 1952

Lewis, C.S., *The Last Battle*, The Bodley Head 1956

Lewis, C.S., *The Lion, the Witch and the Wardrobe*, Lions 1981

Lewis, C.S., *The Weight of Glory*, William Collins 2013

Lewis, Peter, BST, *The Message of the Living God*, Inter-Varsity Press 2000

Merida, Tony, *Exalting Jesus In Exodus*, B&H Publishing Group 2014

Motyer, Alec, BST, *The Message of Exodus*, Inter-Varsity Press 2005

Ogne, Steve & Roehl, Tim, *TransforMissional Coaching*, B & H Publishing Group Nashville2008

Oxford Dictionary, Oxford University Press USA 2012

Palgrave, FT, *Palgrave's Golden Treasury*, Collins Classics 1968

Piper, John, Living by Faith in Future Grace, www.desiringgod.org, November 17 2012

Piper, John, *The Pleasures of God*, Mentor Imprint 2013

Quoist, Michel, *Prayers of Life*, Gill and MacMillan Dublin 1969

Sandburg, Carl, American Pulitzer prize-winning poet, 1878–1967

Spearing, A.C. (Editor, Translator), Anonymous Author, *The Cloud of Unknowing and Other Works*, Penguin Classics Paperback 2001

Spearing, A.C., Spearing, Elizabeth, Julian of Norwich (author), *Revelations of Divine Love*, Penguin Classics Paperback 1998

Spurgeon, Charles, "Marah Better Than Elim", sermon 2301,

delivered 26th March 1893
Stott, John, *Life in Christ*, Kingsway Publications Ltd 1991
The New Strong's Exhaustive Concordance of the Bible, Thomas Nelson Publishers 1990
Thompson, Francis, *The Kingdom of God*, Luath Press Ltd 1997

Flyleaf

Life is an adventure, and the journey with the Source of all life is the greatest, most compelling and satisfying adventure of all. It is about exploring and discovering more and more of God and how he defines and shapes our lives. Each step of the way in this adventure beckons us to rise higher in our relationship with him.

In the Bible and throughout history, the great men and women of the Bible often made the request, "Show me your ways, O Lord". The author has always been fascinated by the ways of God, particularly his paradoxical ways. The Lord's logic seems so contrary to the ways of the world. In his ways of doing things, down is up, darkness is a blinding light, vulnerability is strength, loss is gain, death is the portal to life, surrender is the path to victory. The Holy Spirit comes to illumine our lives, yet in his wisdom he can sometimes choose to come to us in disguise, hidden, withdrawing into silence, and even appearing to abandon us. All the ways of the Lord are loving and wise. It is to our benefit to learn his ways so that we can be reassured and encouraged, saving ourselves from unnecessary bewilderment and pain. We shall find ourselves not misinterpreting and wrestling against God's purposes but recognising and embracing his wise and loving will.

It is as if God is saying to us, "I've got specific ways I want you to follow, but to be successful you have to know the unique strengths and qualities of these ways. It will take some time, so plan on investing that time."

The selection of themes reflects the author's own experiences, having been captivated and enthralled for most of his life by His Majesty, the Lord Jesus Christ.

www.ingramcontent.com/pod-product-compliance
Lightning Source LLC
LaVergne TN
LVHW051117080426
835510LV00018B/2084